The Fisherman's Wife

LOVE & MURDER IN PIRATES COVE

INTERNATIONAL BESTSELLING AUTHOR
T N TRAYNOR

This is a work of fiction. Names, characters, businesses, places, events and incidents either are the products of the author's imagination or used in a fictitious manner. Any resemblance to actual persons, living or dead, or actual events is purely coincidental.

The Fisherman's Wife Copyright © T N Traynor 2022 – All rights reserved

The rights of T N Traynor to be identified as the author of this work has been asserted by her in accordance with the Copyright, Designs & Patents Act 1988

No part of this book may be reproduced, or stored in a retrieval system, or transmitted in any form or by any means, electronic, mechanical, photocopying, recording, or otherwise, without the express written permission of the author. Quotes from the book may be used in reviews.

T. N. Traynor
Publishing

Book cover designed by Maria Pagtalunan
mariachristinepagtalunan@gmail.com

First Printed Edition, England June 2022
ISBN: 9798830861748

US English used throughout

Contents

Contents 3
With thanks 4
Book Description 5
Chapter 1 6
Chapter 2 19
Chapter 3 31
Chapter 4 33
Chapter 5 38
Chapter 6 50
Chapter 7 62
Chapter 8 73
Chapter 9 84
Chapter 10 88
Chapter 11 98
Chapter 12 111
Chapter 13 127
Chapter 14 140
Chapter 15 149
Chapter 16 156
Chapter 17 172
Chapter 18 182
Chapter 19 191
Chapter 20 205
Chapter 21 216
Chapter 22 217
Chapter 23 229
Chapter 24 240
Chapter 25 243
Appendix 248
Author Information 251

With thanks

The greatest gift of life is friendship,
And I have received it.

Hubert H. Humphrey

Nigel you are a true friend. You're help and words of advice make my stories so much better. Always in your debt, Tracy

Book Description

THE FISHERMAN'S WIFE, LOVE & MURDER IN PIRATES COVE

1727. A wife with an oppressive husband. A pirate trapped by circumstance. Together they must face their fears and make a break for freedom.

When Connie's parents died, rather than become homeless she accepted a proposal from a fisherman known for his temper. After seven years of marriage and still childless, she is labeled cursed. Her drunken husband brutally punishes her for her failings and Connie retreats into a world of her own.

Seeking his fortune, Eddie finds himself becoming an unwilling pirate. With no way out of Captain Hawkins' clutches, he concentrates on amassing funds to one day buy his freedom. A harsh life takes its toll on a gentle spirit, and he begins to lose himself in the bloodthirsty life of a pirate.

A violent tempest throws hope into both their lives when Eddie is shipwrecked in the fishing bay of Bigbury-on-Sea and ends up on Connie's beach. Will the two of them take their chance at happiness, and if they do, can they outrun the men who want them dead?

A thrilling historical romance novel, *The Fisherman's Wife* is a gripping atmospheric love story!

Chapter 1

Spring, 1727

MIST, CLAMMY AND EERIE, covered the Devon coastline, and gripped Bigbury-on-Sea in its swirling fingers of biting cold. Connie tightened her shawl around her shoulders as she rushed across the wild plateau. An oil lamp swung in her right hand; its dim yellow flicker did nothing to pierce the fog and failed dismally to illuminate her footpath. The tide would just be out far enough for her to walk the wet sands to Burr Island. She hurried, she needed to be atop the island before sunrise, for Joseph had been nominated this week's huer and he'd sent her to do his job this morning. If she missed a shoal of pilchards, the villagers would show their displeasure, and her husband would reward her with more than harsh words. It would be Joseph's fault if she missed them, for he hadn't allowed her to sleep in the old temple building that the fishermen used as a lookout hut. Although if she was honest, she'd been glad not to spend the night within a hundred yards of the infamous crew who slept aboard their ship hidden in front of the island's sheer cliff face, and the captain of the Flying Angel, Smiley, who slept at the inn.

The sea spray dampened her face and clothes, freezing–yet exhilarating! If only she didn't have a husband, she would be more than content with her lot in life. "Blooming fiend!" she muttered as her feet landed on firmer sand, indicating she'd reached the edge of the raised islet that had been claimed by

Captain Smiley and his pirates. Unofficially, of course, for the Excise Guard Bobby Griffin was paid a pretty penny to look the other way.

She hurried passed the Pilchard Inn, her well-oiled leather boots making no sound, hoping and praying to go unobserved by the Captain and his life-hardened men. A light shone dimly through the rear room's window, meaning someone was awake. She shivered. "Please, let it only be Polly who is afoot this early hour," she pleaded with the mist. There was a healthy respect that must be paid to pirates, but as for their captain she felt nothing but outright dread. When she turned the corner at the top, she allowed herself a sigh, for no shout had hailed her. She raced on to the lookout point. Already the glorious promise of morning was dispersing night's darkness. Yesterday evening's red sky had pledged a day full of sunshine, and she couldn't wait for it to hasten to fullness and warm her cold and bruised bones.

Sure-footed and confident, she hastened to the highest point, only yards away from the cliff's edge, and set the lamp down. Pale light crept over the horizon, pulling itself up with agonizing slowness. "Come on, come on, oh please be a bountiful day!" She searched the waters through the thinning puffs of mist, watching for that discoloration that announced the arrival of fish. "Please come today, please come." Desperate for a day of respite from Joseph's temper, she searched the sea with pounding heart. A full net would mean payment, which in turn meant a visit to the tavern for him and a measure of peace for her.

The lump of raised rock that was Burr Island, sat in the sea with a sense of belonging. The small island appeared like a lobster, its claws spread forward and to the sides, its head held high, with body sloping gently down towards the sands behind it.

It posed with an attitude that emitted both a belonging and a constant challenge against its lifelong friend the sea. For thousands of years, waves had crashed against it, but it remained unmoved, still, and clinging to a heritage of ancient sanctuary and whispered prayers. Solidly ensconced between Earth's core and Heaven it reminded those who trod upon its back that they were fleeting whereas it was eternal. If it wasn't for its current occupancy of pirates, Connie would have enjoyed the rush of the sea swell as it smashed into the runtish island, and the invigorating touch of the sea breeze.

With numb feet and chilled fingers, she wrapped her arms around her body and appealed to the sky for a blessing. Time ticked by. The mist began to disperse. The sun pushed its head over the horizon and rays of light bounced over choppy waters piercing the remaining sea-mist and pushing it aside. Seagulls woke and flew from crags in the cliffs, cawing and squawking and filling the silence with their familiar screams.

"There!" She shielded her eyes and concentrated. "Yes, yes!" Her heart soared with relief. She reached down, picked up the lamp and began swinging it from side to side. Joseph and the other fishermen would see the light from the cliff and beach and know the pilchards had come to the cove today. She alternated between swinging the lamp and cupping her hands over her mouth and calling out, "Here-by, here-by." She carried on until her arm ached and her throat parched. Finally, when she was sure the fishermen couldn't have missed her signal and call she lifted the glass door of the lamp and blew out the wick. She dropped her arm in relief.

"Thank you," she whispered to the ocean. Sitting down on a damp piece of moss and grass, she drew her knees up and hugged them tight to her chest. She would wait awhile, with light and a low tide she would be able to climb down the rocks and run to the shore without having to pass the inn again.

Resting her chin on her knees, Connie smiled at the sea and fell into her constant daydream, the one where she was a widow and as far away from this fishing village as she could get. Freedom was what she dreamed of, and yearned for with the intensity that other women yearned for children. Deep in her core dwelt a glimmer of hope, where it came from she knew not. Most of the time, it remained hidden, dormant, like a heavy sleeper. Which allowed her to live her days with an absence of feelings. But when she had moments like this, it bloomed and opened her spirit to pleasant daydreams and hopeless wishes. Connie couldn't fathom why hope didn't shrivel and die. She was glad of its company though, for with it she built great dreams and lived many lives, all of which saw her as a single woman and hundreds of miles away from Devon and the people who knew her. In these moments of escape, she never saw herself as happily married or a mother. The first was impossible and the second a burden she would never carry. She wanted to be a bird and fly away; to be free – nothing more, nothing less.

Around the edge of the island, five fishing boats glided through the undulating cresting waves, their oars rising and falling in harmony from their years of practice and experience. The men called to each other, and she could hear their urgency and excitement and concluded it must be a large catch. The boats formed a semi-circle, stretching their colossal seine net between them, its tiny mesh perfectly designed to catch the small fish.

She stood up and started the climb down off the island. She would have about two hours to get her chores done before she had to head to the beach to help with the catch.

As she raced back across the sandbar, she wondered what it would be like to keep running and never stop. Once, she had attempted to run away from Joseph. She hadn't gotten far before he'd found her. She could hardly move for a week after the beating he'd given her. Yet it was the look in his eyes when he told her he would kill her rather than let her leave that evoked terrifying dread in her soul. He'd meant those words. He wouldn't hesitate to carry them out, of that she was sure. She shook her head to chase the thought of running away right out of it. Her sandy-blonde curls bounced with the shake. She loved her hair, and when Joseph wasn't around, she spent a long time giving it a hundred strokes with the brush the way her mother had taught her. She wanted to weep whenever she touched the small bald patch she had behind her right ear, in the place where *he* had pulled her hair so violently it had come out and never regrown.

"Monster!" she screamed into the breeze. Under her breath she cursed him. "One day you will be gone, and I will be free. I don't know how or when, but as God is my witness, one day I will be free of you, Joseph Boyton husband of mine!"

Her quick pace soon carried her across the sleepy vale to their humble home. Unlike the other fishermen, who lived in a row of white-washed stone houses not far from the shore, they lived in an old farmhouse set on its own in the sweeping exposed plateau above the village, tucked into the embrace of a few sparse trees, yet still close enough to hear the roar of the sea. There hadn't been an application of the chalked lime here to whiten the building's gray stones in many years, whether her husband was too mean with his coin or too lazy to bother she didn't know. But the lack of a protective wash meant their home had mildew thriving in every corner. It flung a musky scent over everything that was impossible to erase no matter how hard she cleaned.

Connie went first to the chicken run to feed her small brood, and to see if any had laid eggs overnight. For the third day in a row, no eggs were found. After firmly planting her hands on her hips, she scalded the thin birds, "Joseph will have you in the cooking pot mighty soon if you don't start laying again!" The four clucked, pecked, strutted, and appeared deaf to her warning. She didn't have the coin to buy the corn they needed to be productive, and it saddened her heart that Joseph would be for killing them soon.

With a sigh, she went on to her vegetable patch to see what she could pull up for today's dinner. She was struggling this year to produce much and each lack of bountiful crop meant her meals took on a plain and repeated version of pottage, which Joseph had nothing but complaints about. Of course, if he had been a typical fisherman, he would have provided, and brought home a variety of food from the sea, but alas he'd rather spend time playing cards in the tavern. She dug out an onion and two small potatoes and decided she would prepare pease-soup... again. She would flavor it with rosemary, and maybe if the haul was large enough today she'd be able to bring home a handful of pilchards.

The meal simmered in the pot over the peat fire, and the two rooms of their home were cleaned to the best of her ability. Keeping her apron on, she donned her warm woolen cloak and set off for the seafront once more.

Her timing was slightly out today, as the fishermen had already returned to shore and the villagers had finished emptying the catch into stout barrels. She quickened her pace. The whole village was there, men, women and children, taking the fish out of the barrels and repacking them in layers of salt into traveling crates. One look at the crowd told her that Mr. Willoughby had already arrived. She moaned; there would be no sneaking a pilchard or two into her apron pockets today. The tall, lanky landowner strutted as only a man who thought himself important could do. His short black periwig having seen better days, as usual kept slipping to one side. This constant battle with its positioning afforded him the nickname '**Wiggly Willoughby**.' He made a point of walking up and down counting the boxes and recording a note of their weight. His stride was long, his voice sharp. How everyone put up with him she knew not. The net was his of course, none of the fishermen could afford such a thing, only a man to the manor born could, but he might have paid them a little more. She took off her cloak and rolled up her sleeves.

"You're late, lass," said Winifred Hooper with a kindly smile.

"I know, I didn't think they would be so quick, I thought it a large shoal."

"Unfortunately not."

The salt stung her cut and grazed hands and her eyes smarted, she squeezed them tight not wanting to cry in front of everyone. The villagers worked together, emptying, salting and repacking. As time wore on, her back began to ache from the bending and she marveled at how old Winifred managed. As they drew to a close, one of the fishermen struck up a song. They allowed him the first verse on his own, for his voice was mellow and pleasant indeed, then slowly, one-by-one, the others joined in. They sang of the fruits of the sea, of sun and storm, of love and loss, but no matter what verse they were on the tune remained the same up and down chant which meant they could be singing anything and no one would care, for a sea-chant was a sea-chant whatever the lyrics.

At the end, when Mr. Willoughby's carts were loaded up, he paid the men. The women and children were given nothing except a few pilchards that had missed the salting buckets, ones Mr. Willoughby considered too small for market. Joseph didn't even acknowledge Connie when he received his wage; he simply headed for the tavern and his well-earned ale. Other fishermen gave coin to their wives, who looked on Connie with pitying glances, as their husbands also made haste for the inn. She waited until everyone but the seagulls had left the beachfront.

The gulls wheeled overhead and nose-dived into the fishing area now empty of men to chase them away. They swooped in frenzy dives, a menace of gray and white feathers and beaks, irritatingly daring. Their squawks seemed vicious as Connie tried to dissuade them from coming to the spot where she had kicked a large pilchard, under the cover of an overturned rowing boat. She poked her hand under, while batting off a bird with her other hand.

"Mine!" she yelled at it, and finally relenting, the bird turned and hopped away. "Blasted gulls!" she muttered, as she pulled out her stolen booty. She shoved the larger fish into her apron pocket with two other minuscule ones she'd been allowed to take, and pushing against the boat she got up with a moan. It had been a long day. As she straightened she saw the vicar's wife Margaret Neale, observing her. Connie flushed. Mrs. Neale smiled and nodded at her. Connie grabbed her cloak and fled, she wanted no one's pity.

Today Connie had a bounce in her step. Joseph, as he tended to do when he'd partaken of too much drink, had not come home. This meant her night had gone undisturbed and she was well-rested. Oh, that she had money to pay the barman to put her husband in a drunken stupor every day, she would have paid most handsomely! Stepping forward with determination, Connie made her way across the grasslands and headed for the shoreline. Along this way, she hoped to encounter a rabbit or even two as their warrens ran all along the coastal trail. She'd left her cloak behind, for the sun was bright and the breeze not too cool, plus her everyday brown dress enabled her to blend in better than the pale blue of her cloak. In her hand she carried her sling, with which she was an expert shot, and if prey came close enough, she would take home a proper meal.

Connie had patience, so when she was sure she'd come across an active burrow she sat down, found a comfortable position and waited. Keeping her body perfectly still, she allowed her eyes to wander out to sea and daydreams rushed in to greet her. "Not today," she sighed. She had not the energy for believing in something impossible. Luck was with her today, as some days it was not, and after a long wait, a family of rabbits had come out to play.

Heading for home, carrying the dead animal by its ears, Connie was surprised to spot Polly heading her way.

"Ahoy there," waved Polly, who stopped walking and waited for Connie to approach.

In Connie's mind, Polly was a character straight off the page of some wondrous adventure book – maybe from Shakespeare's The Tempest or Miguel de Cervantes' Don Quixote. Some character that bloomed larger than life, for here was a lady that would punch anyone who called her such. Polly Pretty-lips-hits-with-her-fists (or Polly Fists for short), was first and foremost a pirate, secondly she was the partner of Captain Smiley. She stood a towering figure of feminine strength, a head and shoulders above Connie, (who was particularly tall herself for a woman). She was dressed in thigh-high boots, breeches, a tight-fitting leather waistcoat that sat over a frilly, flouncy white shirt and over them a long loose-fitting coat. Her long black hair, tied in a pigtail by a piece of string, flowed out from under her tri-cornered hat, and tucked under her thick leather sash two pistols sat with the confidence of being well-handled and worn in.

"What brings you off the island?" asked Connie as she came alongside her friend of the past year.

"A message for you."

"Me?" A sense of dread washed over Connie as she anticipated the following statement from the only pirate she trusted.

"Joseph told Smiley that you'll tend the bar this evening."

She could kill him. If only it wasn't illegal to bash your husband over the head with an axe or hammer she'd be out back now practicing her swings! "Is there something afoot?" She knew of course there would be. She'd only been asked to work there once before since the pirates arrived last year, and that was during a meeting of smugglers, when they'd told the normal barmaid not to attend – it was something she didn't want to repeat. Joseph deliberately involved her, making her as culpable as the pirates in their dishonest adventures.

"Aye, there is. And, as you know, you can lose your tongue for talking about it. Smiley says you're to come before dark."

There was no point in arguing. Polly was merely the messenger, and against Joseph she could not raise her voice or proclaim her displeasure. "Will you come in for a while?"

"Aye, reckon I will."

Back at the farmhouse, Connie automatically dished Polly a bowl of pottage. Sitting down on a stool outside the door, she started to skin the rabbit. After Connie's third long sigh, Polly burst out laughing.

"Oh come on, surely your life isn't so bad?"

Connie cocked her head to the side and frowned at the pirate, who had finished the food already and pulled out a stool and sat opposite her.

Wide legged, Polly put her elbow on her knee and leaned forward. "I've seen women in far worse positions than yourself, you know." She fiddled with her long clay pipe, lit it, and took a good chuff.

"Seriously?" Connie doubted it.

"Your view of the world is small Connie Boyton, I think it would shock you to see the lives some people live. Even I would have exchanged my life with yours years ago, and done it gladly and gratefully."

Connie didn't believe her, and her face mirrored her thoughts.

"So, let me tell you how Smiley saved my life…"

Without waiting for permission, Polly told her sad story, one that she rarely told anyone. How from the orphanage she had been turned over to the whorehouse at the age of nine. How a husband's infrequent beatings were nothing compared to the monstrosities that some men required of particular women. How, when at last she could take it no more, she had stabbed a man in the neck and been sentenced to penal transportation to serve a life sentence.

"If I'd lived and reached the colonies on that ship, I would have died slowly in the hands of blackguards. That, lassie, is a far worse life than the one you now have. Your man is an oaf, huge I'll grant you, but an oaf nonetheless. His strikes come from a dim mind, and trust me when I tell you; a sharp-minded man inflicts much worse pain." Polly sniffed, and wiped her nose with her sleeve. "There are some men that delight in torture, now those men you should fear. I have known a couple that made me wish to end my life! If Smiley hadn't captured the ship and set me free I shudder to think of what would have followed. He saved me, in more ways than one."

"Is that why you love him, because he rescued you?" She wanted to add, 'despite his blood-lust and murderous ways' but refrained.

"Aye, I suppose, but 'tis more than that really. He loves me in his own way. He says he's grown used to sleeping against my curves, that's his way of showing affection. And to be honest, my love is enough for the two of us. You see a pirate who must be feared, I see a man longing for a different life."

Connie wasn't convinced. "Don't you ever wish for something more?"

"Wishes are worthless. You can no more live on a wish as you can live under the sea. Wishes are for fools, remember that well." Polly stood up and stretched, taking a deep breath. "This air is so fresh here; if you lived in London for a while you'd stop breathing for the air is putrid there. I'll see you later, and Connie... don't be late."

Connie watched Polly stride away, the woman cared for her as much as her own mother had done, and she knew the warning was for her benefit.

Chapter 2

THEY CAME FROM BUCKLAND, Thurlstone, Sutton, Bigbury, Houghton and other places thereabouts. Fishermen, farmers of land and livestock, honest occupations, normal folk, people she had known all her life and liked well enough. With hats pulled low and coats raised to their chins, they scurried furtively, desiring to remain naught more than shadows in the night.

For all their secret deployment, Connie knew what they were about. Smugglers, one and all, come to plan the next shipment. Some came to satisfy greed's demands, but most participated in the illegal activity to feed their families and keep their homes. For what is a man to do when farming and fishing no longer provide enough for their needs? This united them in a common cause. *Darkness* had spread throughout the hills and valleys of this beautiful Devonshire land. It had arrived on the back of hunger, was welcomed and stayed, becoming the only way out. To survive they must do the unthinkable, they must cross a line that would torment their souls forevermore, but cross it they must, and into the Pilchard Inn they came one-by-one. Survival instincts squashed principles and morality. This band of everyday men joined as one in pursuit of shipwrecking and smuggling. There was no choice and no turning back once they had set upon this course and joined the band of pirates in the cove of Bigbury-on-Sea. Their shanties from this day forth would be droll and full of sorrow, for farmers and fishermen both had become reluctant shipwreckers and pirates' friends.

Connie stood on the edge of the rocks and held the lantern high, a beacon for those who hurried to the meeting. Her cloak hood was low over her face, pulled low, putting her face in the shade of the light. But peeking out from beneath it she could clearly see the shadows of the men who hurried across the causeway.

Strangers mixed with familiar faces. Keeping their gaze set upon the sand they hurried by with as much stealth as they could muster.

Someone called out to her as he approached, "Watch out for the ghost of Tom Crocker!" The man laughed as he rushed by.

"Long way off till the 13th of August, sure I'll be fine!" Her remark only caused the man to chuckle some more.

Smiley had chosen a good night, for the moon lay hidden behind racing clouds casting the land behind them into dark shadows. With the tide on the way out they would have a few hours for their meeting.

"Do any more come?" she called to a man who rushed towards Burr Island so fast, his cloak flew behind him, though he kept a grip of its hood low over his face.

"Nay, I waited to ensure no more approached before I set off, I be the last today."

She recognized the voice but could not put a name to it. As soon as he had passed her, she followed behind, went up the slope and entered the inn.

What an atmosphere there was tonight! The bellow of Smiley's laughter rumbled across their heads, causing many to laugh without knowing the cause of it. Never had she known a man both chalk and cheese, so capable of violence and yet so amenable when he took a care. It was indeed as if Captain Smiley had one day come upon Mr. Jackman Dawe (his former self) and swallowed him whole, two becoming one and each struggling for control.

The villagers' laughter that followed his laugh was cracked, wild, forced and lacking in genuine mirth. It was a chilling sound, that acknowledged weak men's fear, and it was appalling to Connie's ears.

Old Jimmy Peg-Leg was leaning on the wooden counter, deep in conversation with Vera Brave. She laughed at something he said before going to find a seat. Jimmy's wooden stump, which replaced his leg from the knee down, knocked loudly as he moved around and served up drinks. No coin exchange took place, all barrels of ale and bottles of brandy had come from Smiley's private stash to oil the conscience of Bigbury folk.

Connie cast her eye over the contrast between normal folk and pirate, as she set to filling pewters full of ale. There emanated from the pirates a certain mettle, a strange aura that enabled them to lay their heads on piracy's pillow of life without a second thought. Life's hardened souls, where no place in respectable society had been set aside for them. How strikingly flamboyant they appeared compared to the drab apparel of land workers and fishermen. Bright colored bandannas or woolen caps covered their heads, their leathers and cloths brightened by jewels plated into beards, bracelets and necklaces. Every pirate had come armed with several daggers, pistols and some even a cutlass. She knew they didn't always carry their weapons and finery on them and that this evening it was for show, a declaration and a reminder to all that they were pirates, every last one of them.

Smiley sat in his usual place next to the fire, with his back against the dark-stone wall, his black cat Queenie curled into a ball on his lap. The fire burned bright and high, yellow flames jumping up the granite chimney. The air hung thick with pipe smoke which bounced off the low wooden ceiling. As men slunk into the inn, he sat and picked at his teeth with his nail. "Polly," he yelled, "I've a thirst on me all the water of the Avon will not quench, where's me grog?"

Polly rushed to his side with a tumbler of rum in one hand and a pitcher of beer in the other.

"Come on Polly Pretty-Lips-hits-with-her-fists, we're all waitin' on bein' served," cooed Snake-Eye.

"Polly Fists, to you Snake-Eye, and if you don't use me right name, I'll use me fists and leave you with no good eyes!"

The pirates about them laughed and smacked Snake-Eye on the back. He sneaked a quick glance at Smiley. When he saw the captain watching him closely, he grinned and acted the good-natured fool he was not. "Oh, you be leavin' me one good eye alone, Polly Fists, I'll not be calling you out again."

Polly turned her back on him and returned to the bar, her hips swaying behind her. If she had been in a dress rather than breeches, it would have swished from left to right.

Connie handed out drinks to the landlubbers and fishermen and as much as possible avoided Smiley, though she could feel his eyes on her often. Joseph was sitting in a corner, and when she handed him a drink he snarled at her to keep them coming.

Joseph was almost a head-and-shoulder taller than the other men. With broad shoulders and large hands he was the fisherman they all wanted in their boat, but on land he was the drunk they wanted to be sitting at another table.

"Your husband is in love with the devil drink, it'll probably kill him one of these days and then you'll get your longed-for freedom."

Connie looked up at Polly who had just whispered that to her with a heavy wink. "I'm bound to my man by law, but why do you stay with Smiley when there's no contract between you? He also drinks too much, and I'm sure he's even meaner than Joseph when he's drunk. I've seen your bruises Polly; you can't hide them from me!"

"He drinks like a fish and has the temper of the Devil himself, but he's my devil Connie, and I love him true." Polly's loving gaze towards the pirate was beyond Connie's understanding; she could not imagine ever loving a man like that, especially a man with blood on his hands.

Smiley was known for his missing front teeth, the absence of which was unmissable when he smiled. With his incisors missing, his canines appeared overly long and dreadfully pointed. Despite his lack of front teeth, his grin was wolfish and deceitful. An angry scar ran from the right side of his mouth along the lower part of his right cheek. It served to appear almost as an extension of his mouth, which in turn made his smiles and snarls alike horrific. The scar often gave him the appearance that he was always smiling. This, an outright lie, for Captain Smiley hardly ever smiled. He occasionally laughed; big barking honks that streamed in triplets – ha-ha-ha! Followed by silence until the next burst… ha-ha-ha. The laughter flowed from his belly with deep booms and shook his body. Despite his cutthroat personality, when he laughed it was infectious and those around him laughed without knowing the cause, but not Connie. She held before her always the tales she'd been told of his cutthroat ways and she would not be deceived by his attempt at being good-natured.

Bang, bang, bang.

Smiley knocked his fist against the wooden table, Queenie jumped from his lap and ran off, and the room hushed into silence. "Welcome to the meeting of shipwreckers and smugglers!"

The newcomers remained silent; the pirates roared and raised their cups.

"On the table here," he gave the table another bang. "Lays our contract, before we begin with our plans everyone must sign. Everyone!" When no one moved, Smiley dragged back his chair and stood up. "My name has already been put, and so have the names of all my men, if you want in, you will put your mark or leave! For I swear by the memory of Tom Crocker here..." he slapped a flat hand against an eerie image that people professed was the impression left by Tom when he'd been shot on this very spot. "By my smuggling friend here," he tapped the image. "I promise you it's for your own good that you jump lively and come sign your mark. Or you'd best batten down your hatches and hope I don't find 'ee!"

Slowly, they got up from their stools and came to put their names, or a cross, on Smiley's contract. When the last was signed, he nodded and sat back down. "Good, I would not have liked to get my dagger dirty tonight by slitting one of your throats!" Several fishermen and farmers gulped, Connie nearly dropped the tankard she was washing.

Smiley waved the parchment until the ink had dried, then rolled it and popped it in his jacket breast pocket. "This," he tapped the pocket, "is our bond. It will tie us together in profit, or it will get us all hanged! But be warned, it is our bond and you break it only if you wish both your death and the murder of your family!"

Connie, (who usually never drank) poured some rum into a cup and swigged it back in one go. She immediately coughed. When she looked up, everyone was looking at her.

Smiley removed the paper from his pocket. "It seems we still have one more to sign the contract." Connie's knees weakened. She didn't want to sign, nor did she want to be associated with them. She threw daggers at her husband with her eyes and clenched her fists. Joseph lowered his tankard and fixed his evil eye upon her. She had no choice. She crossed the room, dipped the quill into the ink and signed her name with a flourish. As she straightened and returned to the bar she saw the look of surprise on her husband's face. She smirked, for she knew he didn't know his letters and would have only placed a cross as his mark.

"Now for business," said Smiley, and all attention went his way.

"The rich rob the poor and do so under the cover of the law, but we plunder the rich under the protection of our courage. Pirates are free princes challenging authority, Robin Hoods each and every one of us!"

His crew didn't mind that Smiley had stolen those words from the legacy of Captain Bellamy; after all, Bellamy had been dead these ten years gone and was hardly able to protest. So they raised their cups and cheered.

"I have news that a ship comes. It carries rum, tobacco and French brandy. It will drop anchor and deliver the goods to Bantham."

Murmurs spread throughout the villagers.

Smiley waited for someone to protest. Slowly, a man stood up. He pulled his cap off and wrung it in his hands. "Bantham folk are neighbors, we cannot steal from them. Have you never heard of not fouling where you sleep?"

There was that voice Connie had recognized, and could hardly believe her eyes, for it was none other than the Waiter and Searcher of Bigbury himself, Bobby Griffin!

"There is truth in what you say, and it wouldn't be good to go to war with people who live an arm's length away. However, this is not their ship, nor do the goods belong to them. I am told the stash that is coming was itself stolen from a French galleon recently. They are looking to smuggle most of it to London, and plan to use the tunnels from the caves on Bantham beach up to The Sloop tavern. The blacksmith's forge at Whiddons will hoard it until they can distribute it safely. We are simply stealing from thieves! Once they have it either at The Sloop or in the blacksmith's we will swoop in and take it for ourselves."

Benjamin Hooppell slightly raised his hand to gain attention. "We should go at night when no one is around, that way no one will get hurt. That is your plan isn't it, to get in and out without trouble?"

Smiley rested one hand on the hilt of his cutlass, pushing back his long coat so everyone could clearly see. He was past his best years and had grown plump with their year of little activity, yet he was as formidable now as he'd always been. But Hooppell was born and bred a Bigbury man, and many of his relatives lived on the other side of the River Avon in Bantham, he would not be part of any falling out between them. There were whispers from the fishermen and it was clear they all felt the same.

"We'll wait for the ship to unload and be on its way, and once folk have retired, we'll make our move. I don't want unnecessary trouble with them but... the goods are for the taking, so, are you with me or not?"

The villagers set to whispering between themselves, eventually Hooppell turned to face the pirate. "With the understanding that no one will be hurt, we stand by you."

"So be it. The ferryman has been paid. He will take us back and forth until we have the goods on this side of the river. When we're ready we'll cart the goods to Totness, there I have men who will take them on to London."

"And how do we know you will share your payment with us?" asked Bobby Griffin. All eyes turned to Smiley, waiting for the answer that was on every one of their minds.

"A pirate is bound by his word, and I give you my word you will all be paid, and with more than a Sloop coin!"

After the villagers had left, the pirates sat around small round tables and slugged their drinks with sober melancholy. It should not matter what others thought of them, but they themselves felt the loss of their 'feared' status. It carried an air of decline from which none of them would ever be able to rise. If the sea was not their mistress, and landlubbers no longer lived in fear of them, well by-Jove life had lost its luster.

"Listen," said Smiley. "When we were seamen and paid an honest coin we could lift our heads high. But when the war finished and we were no longer employed in the service of war or offered comfortable bread, what recourse did we have but to follow necessity and take our needs by dishonest means?" There were hearty agreements from around the small room.

"When we were men who straggled and begged all over the kingdom, why should any be amazed when crime became our only opportunity? We moved from the Pirate's Commonwealth which has had its day and died, but we are still bound together by Pirate's Oath and we'll continue to share our booty in a manner fair to all."

There came a polite 'yeah' to his statement but he knew their hearts weren't in it. They had lived a life of kings, in their private kingdom on the ocean. Now they had turned to smuggling, which involved moving goods under the eye of the coast guards and customs men. It would not be so easy to avoid the hangman's noose when the red coats could be all around them.

Some pirates pulled their hats low over their foreheads; one tapped his empty pipe against his palm with unconscious beats. Another wrapped his arm around his mate, and yet another coughed to disperse the lump formed in his throat.

"There's good gain in smuggling, men," bellowed Smiley.

They halfheartedly responded by lifting their mugs and nodding their heads. Smiley fixed his gaze upon a French pirate by the name of Pierre Baudelaire, or 'Little Daggers' as he was called, who was renowned for the destruction of many a female reputation! Partly attributed to his dashing good looks of jet-black hair and piercing blue eyes, partly because he had a husky voice that simply made women swoon. His dulcet accent was hypnotizing, and no more so than when he sang.

"Little Daggers," called Smiley. "Give us a tune."

Little Daggers swept off his hat and gave an exaggerated flourish of a bow towards his captain. He picked up his cittern that had lain in wait propped against the wall, and swung the strap over his neck and shoulder. The room fell silent, all eyes shifted to the colorful persona of the little French man.

He strummed a few chords, appeared to think for a moment, and when his eyes lit up with an idea, he smiled at them all.

Fare you well my dear, I must be gone
And leave you for a while
If I roam away I'll come back again
Though I roam ten thousand miles, my dear
Though I roam ten thousand miles

So fair thou art my bonny lass
So deep in love am I
But I never will prove false to the bonny lass I love
Till the stars fall from the sky my dear
Till the stars fall from the sky

The sea will never run dry, my dear
Nor the rocks never melt with the sun
But I never will prove false to the bonny lass I love
Till all these things be done my dear
Till all these things be done

O yonder doth sit that little turtledove
He doth sit on yonder high tree
A making a moan for the loss of his love
As I will do for thee my dear
As I will do for thee

The pirates roared their approval, and Little Daggers received many a hearty slap on the back. Connie washed the pots and kept her thoughts to herself; but she was plagued by the inkling that Smiley had hidden something from everyone this evening.

When at last the pirates had taken their fill of booze, they bid the captain a good rest, and using the tunnels under the inn, made their way back to the caves at the front of the island, and onto their ship the Flying Angel.

Little Daggers blew the angel figurehead a kiss as he went past her to the gangplank. "Sleep well my belle fille."

Chapter 3

"WHY AM I HERE?" she screamed at the waves.

Sunlight glistened and merrily danced upon cresting white horses, a million hooves thundering to the shore, but they didn't offer her an answer. "My life's nothing but drudgery and pain. I don't understand my reason for being." Anger at the world for dealing her such a harsh hand wrestled with her desire to be at peace. "Mothers at least have children to love, men their ale and old-dog tales. What about me?"

Waves lapping on the shore crept forward as if to touch her feet. If she could embrace the ocean she would. Whether turbulent or still it called to her soul. She should have been a mermaid, swimming beneath the surface, wild and free. "Oh, sea, I love you well, but no warm embrace or kind word can you offer me in return for my adoration. What a selfish lover you make! And yet... when I'm with you I'm awed by your presence, and that I'm nobody except myself when I'm with you. How little and insignificant you make me appear. Oh, crashing waves, how you stir my soul and thrill my spirit so! I take it back, what a great lover you are! Eternally giving, and never taking."

The wind picked up and blew her curls behind her, making her skirts dance, and causing the sea to crash with a little more power. Her eyes shifted from the breakers on the shore to the horizon. Black clouds, thick and clustered, raced towards land. She gauged the distance and speed, and estimated she had less than an hour before rain soaked the land.

"There's a storm a-brewing, that's for sure."

She made her way up the narrow track she'd cut for herself in the cliff face, for this beach was inaccessible during high tide and had become her secret haven. She came here to hide from the world, but mostly from Joseph. He never found her here, for everyone thought the cliff unyielding and nothing but a death trap. She liked to dice with death though; she wouldn't complain if it sneaked up on her and stole her last days. She was halfway up the cliff face when the wind picked up speed. Clinging on to her stepping rocks, she turned slightly and looked out to sea. The black clouds had thickened and darkened.

"You're a harbinger of trouble if ever there was one!" As she continued her climb, she thought about the ship that was to arrive soon. How if it came now, the storm would hide the wicked plans set against it, its hoard, and their neighbors in Bantham. She shivered, and not from the cold.

Chapter 4

ONE-EYED CAPTAIN HARRY HAWKINS – Hawk-Eye to his crew, determined that today was not his day to die!

"To your posts, you damn sea-dogs!" he bellowed from behind the helm. Another wave tilted them sideways and he grabbed the wheel with all his might. Screams and crashes sounded from every quarter, and he saw Sam Mountain – a formidable African man he had freed from slavery, grab hold of the pint-sized Italian quartermaster Giovanni Luigi Fontana (who no nickname had been given to, as he was rather fond of hearing his own name) and stopped him from being washed overboard. When the sloop keeled again, Hawkins knew the old man-of-war Rosalie, had seen her last days, yet he called for the men to turn sail and to try and right her.

Eddie hissed under his breath. Trying to save the sloop was a preposterous sentence that would see them all dashed upon the rocks, they should be looking to escape before she sunk and took them all with her. Yet the men trembled at the captain's severity and obeyed without hesitation, traversing the deck with disordered steps. With mood of doom and gloom they ran, slipped and tumbled, and made every effort to bring the sloop to obedience and into safe harbor.

The main mast was the first to go. The sodden sail weighing it down until it creaked and snapped with a sound that all the men recognized as fatal. Snapped and trailing in the sea the mast relinquished the sail to the ocean, where it floated like a sea-witch's hair, horrifying, yet to Eddie somewhat hypnotizing as well. A thought came to him... there would be no survivors from this wreck. The sea was too violent, too gloriously bad-tempered to care for the bodies of men that were as insignificant as grains of sand and would be tossed about with complete indifference.

"Prepare to abandon ship!" yelled Hawkins at last through cupped hands.

Eddie, hanging onto the third mast for dear life, heard the captain's yell and made a swift decision.

"Where you going, Earnest Eddie?" said Hawk-Eye to himself, as he spied his boatswain diving for the cabins. Realization dawned, "Oh, no you don't you thieving snake!" Hawkins let go of the wheel and made a lurch forward to follow his boatswain.

The storm had sprung from nowhere. At first the squall had seemed as moderate as May weather might be. But once they were in the center of it, all hell had broken loose. First, the main mast had snapped in two. That alone was bad news. Then the anchor had been cut loose and now they had nothing to prevent the ship from being hurled towards the shore and waiting rocks.

As a crew they had recently decided that their piracy days were over. Ten years ago, after King George I's 'Proclamation for Suppressing of Pirates' granted full pardon of all crimes to pirates who surrendered, things had become intolerable for honest pirates who wanted to plunder without murder. Now it seemed every man and his dog was out to capture them, even former pirates, making plunder without murder impossible. Therefore, they'd agreed to drop The Black, and to offer their services to 'businessmen,' and to become smugglers instead.

How cruel was life? Now that they had made this decision, they were about to lose their sloop and therefore their livelihood.

Eddie Calstock was thinking that very thing, as he made his unsteady way to the captain's cabin. As boatswain, he knew every inch of the ship, including where Hawkins had stashed their treasure cache of gold doubloons. The ship was sinking, and he'd be damned if he let their wealth go down with it. As he entered through the door into the captain's cabin, the sloop groaned and began a tilt that threw Eddie sliding across the floor, trying desperately to hold onto something. Creaks and groans, and a moment's steadiness, and then an almighty thud announced their doom. Eddie swore as the ship smashed into rocks. Holding onto to the frame of the room, he pulled himself around to the captain's bunk. Water flooded in, a freezing deluge that soon reached the height of his knees. For a brief moment, he considered fleeing, but instead he gritted his teeth and lunged at the secret compartment hidden under the bunk.

At first it wouldn't open. Eddie began to panic; he was running out of time. He hammered the panel, again and again until eventually it split and he was able to pull the rest away with his bare hands. All the while he could hear his shipmates screaming as they were tossed overboard, dashed on the rocks, or were struck by flying debris. He yanked the small chest out and turned for the door. The ship was now fully on its side and the cold salty water was up to his waist. He waded across the room and looked at the door with some dismay. It was several feet above him. He searched for a way out.

"Be calm!" he ordered himself. But his hands, that held his loot, were shaking. "I'll not be drowned like a rat."

In that exact moment, the head of Sam Mountain appeared in the doorway. They looked at each other and grinned.

"You be sharing that, Earnest Eddie?"

"Aye, of course, it belongs to us all. I'm simply looking out for the crew."

Sam Mountain didn't believe the boatswain for a moment, but the man had saved his life and more than once. He lowered a rope. "You don't have long, Earnest Eddie."

Eddie now chest-deep in water grabbed the cord from the bunk's drapes and used it to tie the box to his chest. He took hold of the rope Sam offered him with both hands and started hauling himself up. By the time he reached the door, the cabin was nearly fully submerged. He looked at Sam, but they had no time for him to give thanks. They turned to see which way off the splintering ship would offer the safest route. As they did so, Hawkins crashed into them. The three of them slipped to onto their backsides and slid across the remaining parts of the sloop.

There was another almighty groan, and the ship went down. Eddie lost sight of both Sam and Hawkins as he jumped as far out as he could. He sank into the biting cold. Down and down he went. He saw Jacob floating, arms wide and eyes wider. Down and down he went. Crates scattered everywhere. He started kicking, but he was heavy. He kicked and pushed the water with his arms as he fought his way towards the surface. He couldn't make it. To get to the air he would have to release the chest from his body. He wanted the coins within this box, he really did, but he wanted to live more. His fingers started fumbling with the knot. He couldn't undo it. He continued kicking and glanced around him for help. There was none.

The current knocked him into a part of the broken ship, his arms flung out. His lungs were bursting. Forgetting about the box he tried one more time for the surface. But the sea was playing with the pirate; it picked him up in a current and catapulted him upon jagged rocks. Pain exploded in his leg and he forgot he was under water and opened his mouth to scream. Water rushed in. He knew no more. His body surrendered to the sea and his world went blank.

Chapter 5

THE EYE OF THE STORM hit later that night. No call had reached them that the expected ship approached, and eventually Joseph had settled in bed. He was already snoring; his drunken stupor would not be interrupted if all the skies fell upon him. Only a bucket of cold water would be able to rouse him to attend with the smugglers should they call for him. Connie was free to go and enjoy the tempest. Thunder and lightning crashed around her, the white streaks of light both exhilarating and petrifying. She counted between the ear-splitting booms. Lightning lit up the sky. "One buttercup, two buttercups, three buttercups..." She jumped when the crash of thunder sounded as if right behind her. Three miles away and approaching fast. Lashing, pitiless rain stung her face and hands. Laughter burst out of her, making her sound crazy, which made her laugh all the more. She abandoned all hope of trying to keep her dress dry, and let the wind whip her hood back and let go of the edges of her cloak, so it billowed in the wind like bat wings. If any saw her they would say they had seen a madwoman racing to her doom, as she ran towards the cliff's edge. But she had never cared what people thought, their opinion of her meant nothing, except when it caused Joseph to lose his temper.

At the edge she pulled her soaked cloak around her, and stood looking at the enormous waves crashing against the shore, endlessly battering the beach with their anger and deafening roar.

Her heart pounded with strenuous throbs. She was in her favorite place, at one with nature. Life pulsed through her blood making her the most awake she'd ever been. All of a sudden, she caught sight of a fluttering shadow on the rolling waves.

The ship had arrived! "Oh Lord, but it'll surely perish." She looked towards the village. Not only did pale flickering lights seep from homes, but a line of lights led to the beach. They knew already. Her heart sank. No red coats had been near Bigbury-on-Sea for months, leaving the Waiter and Searcher of Bigbury – the dishonest Bobby Griffin, to turn a blind eye. This wouldn't be a procession of people eager to help; this would be opportunists looking for the spoils from a sinking ship. "If I could warn you I would," she called out to the ship that was tilting towards destruction.

Lightning lit up the sky, a spotlight of doom over the ship. The galleon seemed to right itself momentarily, and then with horrific slowness, it was shunted against rocks. The sound split the air almost as loudly as the nearby thunder. Above the storm she heard the wood creak and groan. Worse than that… she listened to the screams of men filtering through the din of the storm. Tears poured down her cheeks and mingled with the salty rain. "Oh merciful God, save them!"

She jumped as thunder again roared overhead. It jolted her into action and she started climbing down her secret way to her beloved beach. With the tide on its way out, she would be able to watch the night's horrors from its shores. If someone needed help, she would be his or her only hope. She scrambled too quickly and fell, crashing down on rocks she was normally so sure-footed on. Her head bounced on a rock and she screamed in pain and fright. Lightning lit up the sky as blood trickled down her face, mingling with tears and relentless rain. She forced herself up; she had to get down there. She went more slowly, finding her familiar stones with care before stepping down. Eventually, she reached the comfort of sand and sighed. She pulled a large dock leaf out of a crevice in the cliff and used it to try and mop up some of the blood that had soaked her face. Once done she started searching the beach for survivors. The search was near impossible though, as dark clouds hid the moon and prevented its light reaching the shore. Soon, she realized the current and the positioning of the ship meant the jettison would more likely be washed up on the other side of the small cove, the beach where the villagers swung their lights to beckon unsuspecting survivors. She waited a while to make sure; when nothing washed ashore, she decided she had better go home. She was about to leave when a dark shape in the water caught her attention. She rushed forward and waded into the sea.

It was a man! Face down! The waves rolled him in, desiring to dispose of the body with merciless roughness. Connie went deeper, not caring for her clothes or shoes. She caught hold of him, precisely in the moment when the sea had changed its mind and was dragging him back out again. She turned him over, put her arms under his shoulders and dragged him back to the beach. It proved difficult to pull him out of the water and onto the sand. Fully clothed he was weighted down and almost beyond her capability. She managed to drag him far enough out of the water to prevent him being pulled back in. Panting and out of breath, she dropped to her knees next to his head. Lowering her face, she hovered her cheek over his mouth, waiting to feel his breath.

When no sound or air came forth, she yelled in frustration. "You mustn't die, you mustn't." A memory of watching a woman revive a fisherman who had nearly drowned flooded to the front of her mind. "Yes, yes, I remember!" She started pushing on his chest, forcing the ocean out of his lungs. A spurt of water shot from his mouth, but still he didn't breathe. She did it again, and again water flowed from his mouth. "You will *not* die on me!" she screamed as she pumped his chest with all her might. This time a fountain of water gushed up and out of his lungs, and with it he coughed. "Thank God, oh thank God." She sat back on her heels and looked at her catch. He was breathing but his eyes remained closed. Reaching forward she shook his shoulder. "Wake up."

He didn't stir. It was then that her glance finally traveled over his body. She gasped when she saw his leg. Blood was seeping through his ripped breeches and exposing a deep gash. There was also a gash on his forehead, but although it looked deep, it didn't seem to be bleeding much anymore.

"What am I to do with you?" If she told the villagers about him, she knew he would be murdered. But if she kept him hidden and fetched the custom's men, he would also end up a dead man – swinging from the gallows. For he was a pirate, and of that there was no mistaking. Every inch of his attire had the swagger of a pirate, from his frilled shirt, leather waistcoat and wide silk sash around his waist. Even his coat, that displayed rips no doubt caused by rocks, clearly marked its wearer as a pirate, with big brass buttons and fancy edging. An ornate dagger still nestled under his sash. She pulled it out anxiously, when he didn't move, she jumped up and threw it into the sea.

"So this was Smiley's dastardly plan… to steal from pirates! No wonder he had looked like he had something to hide, she knew it! For if the villagers had known they would have been going up against pirates they would have fled. Now nature had delivered the ship and its bounty into their hands, a gift for the taking.

She looked down at him. What was she to do? She couldn't leave him on the beach, because if he didn't wake when the tide returned it would take him for sure. She glanced towards the sheer cliff face. Pulling him up was an impossible task, what could she do? She bent and shook him roughly.

"Wake up!" she hissed at him.

He didn't stir.

The crashing waves on the shore behind her, reminded her that she was far from help and had positioned herself next to a pirate who might wake at any moment and cut her throat! My, but her mother would have called her a fool, and deserving of the title she would be! She was tempted for a moment to simply leave him to his fate and forget about him, instead she found her gaze fixed upon him. She sat down, pulled his head onto her lap, and covered his face with light slaps. "Wake up," she urged, but he did not stir. As she held his head and gazed upon his face, a strange feeling washed over her, one that must certainly represent the tenderness of motherhood, for she had an urge to tend him and keep him safe. She stroked his cheek. A sense of possession came over her.

She needed help, and the only person she trusted was Polly Fists. She made her mind up; she would fetch Polly. Getting up, she grabbed him under his arms and hauled him backwards across the sand away from the sea, and into the opening of a small cave. Hopefully, he would remain hidden from searching eyes. She walked up and down the cave she knew so well, searching its every corner. Satisfied, she ran to the cliff and scrambled up it as deftly as she could.

Connie raced back to their cottage. Polly would be on the beach with the other looters, and Connie could hardly arrive on the beach without her husband.

The storm, or some sixth sense, must have eroded his sleep because Joseph was just rising when she burst in through the door.

"You've got to come quick, Joseph. You're needed on the beach!"

Knowing of the ship's imminent arrival, Joseph had laid on his bed fully dressed, so now he simply grabbed his coat and shrugged into it. He did up the buttons as they charged to the beach.

"You took your sweet time," snarled the pirate Bill Bones as they arrived.

"We live far back, no one fetched us otherwise we would have come at once," gushed Connie, who immediately strode into the sea to clasp hold of a barrel that floated her way. Hopefully, Joseph in his sleepy stupor wouldn't have noticed she was already drenched through.

Farmers, fishermen, and pirates hauled everything they could find out of the sea and up onto the small, sheltered dock. Connie closed her eyes whenever she saw a body wash up on the beach, and kept praying for their souls and asking their forgiveness for not saving them.

By the time dawn began to light up the sky, the worst of the storm had passed, and the goods had all been stashed in Thomas

Woodmason's boat shed. Connie had tried to turn the other way, but even so she couldn't block out the screams of the survivors as the pirates slit their throats.

"Dead men tell no tales," Smiley kept reminding them, as he marched up and down the beach. The villagers hung their heads and concentrated on carrying the flotsam.

"Clear the beach," cried Smiley, "before its light!"

They needed no encouragement, farmers and fishermen scurried for the comfort of home and family to remind them why they had been on the beach.

Eventually, Connie found herself alone with Polly.

"Can I burden you with a secret, and will you swear on your life not to betray it?" implored Connie with a look over her shoulder and fidgeting hands.

Polly took off her bandanna and shook her hair loose. "Guess 'tis important, if you need me to swear."

"I wouldn't ask it of you, but I know if I share my secret with you, you'll want to tell Smiley, and I need you not to do that. If you are unable to swear I will understand."

Polly looked the sodden Connie up and down. "No, if you need me, I'll swear. I seem to be unable to say no to a drowned rat. What is it?"

Connie cast furtive glances around, realized most had gone, and that no one was near. "Come with me, I'll show you." The two headed off the beach and up the lane to Connie's home. She knew this would give the illusion the two women were going to her cottage. Once they were on the top of the hill and out of sight, Connie back-tracked them to the coastal path.

"Where are we going?"

"You'll see, nearly there."

Polly shook her head as Connie descended over the side of the cliff, but she followed without complaint. When they went around some boulders and approached the cave, Polly saw what lay on the sand. She turned and snapped at her friend. "Are you crazy?"

Connie flew to Polly's side and grabbed her arms. "Please, please don't tell, you promised, you gave me your oath!"

"Curse you for this Connie; you'll get us both killed!"

Connie breathed more easily, Polly wouldn't tell. "We have to move him before the tide comes in."

"And what do you intend to do with him?"

"There's an old shepherd's hut a distance from here. I go there regularly. No one has used it for many a year, I don't even know how it still stands."

"And…" said Polly, pointing to the pirate's leg. "How are we to get him there like that?"

Connie put her hand under her corset and brought out a stretch of linen. "We can use this to bind it, and I thought if he was between us, then maybe we could carry him there?"

"Up the cliff!" Polly snapped. "That's impossible."

"If we could wake him, we could move him from rock to ledge, push and shove, and help him to the top."

"*If…* we can wake him," replied Polly.

Now Connie's heart sank; for this had been her concern all along, that the pirate was on the way to dying and too far gone for waking. She sank on the sand beside him, reached her hand over and gently shook his shoulder. There was no response. If it hadn't been for the gentle rise and fall of his chest she would have feared him already gone.

"You'll never wake him like that," said Polly, and gave him a vicious shove with her boot. This rocked his body slightly and moved his leg, this time he moaned.

After throwing Polly a glare, Connie began shaking the pirate by his shoulders. "Wake up," she urged.

It took some more coaxing, but finally the pirate opened his eyes. Connie sucked in her breath. His glazed eyes showed his confusion, but they were also the brightest sky-blue eyes she had ever seen. Laced with specs of colors his eyes shone like the sun on the crest of waves. She sat back on her heels and stared at him.

"Holy Moses!" chuckled Polly. "Well if he ain't a pretty boy then I've never seen one! No wonder you're so intent on rescuing him!"

In truth, Connie hadn't really paid his looks too much attention before. However, now she couldn't move her gaze away. Long, black lashes framed his stunning eyes. His nose was straight, his lips deep-red and his mustache and chin beard were the same color as his tight-curled hair, a dark brown, sun-kissed in places and tinged with yellow.

"Can you hear me?" she asked eventually.

He gave a very slight nod, and Connie sighed in relief. The gash on his head hadn't addled him as she had feared.

"You need to get up," she urged.

When he made no effort to move, Polly came and stood near his face and frowned down on him. "I reckon we have less than an hour before Smiley and his men start searching the coast for bounty and... survivors."

That roused him. He blinked and tried to roll over. His moan was way too loud, and Polly dropped onto her haunches and hissed in his face. "Do you want to bring them down on us? If not for your own sake you ought to realize we'll both have our throats slit along with yours!"

The pirate nodded, and rolled over again, this time biting his lip and remaining silent.

Once he was sitting up, Connie set to binding his leg with the cloth she had brought from home when she went to get Joseph earlier.

"That'll never hold," said Polly. "Move aside."

Connie moved. Polly knelt and yanked the cloth really tight. The pirate moaned, his eyes released tears but he didn't make a sound louder than a moan.

"What's your name?" Polly asked.

"Edmond Calstock."

"Earnest Eddie, well I live and breathe! Under normal circumstances I would be pleased to make your acquaintance."

"You know him?" Connie asked.

"I know of his reputation," replied Polly. "I'll tell you all I know about it another time. For now, we need to move."

Each woman took Eddie under an arm and helped pull him to his feet. Half hopping and half carrying they got him to the cliff edge in no time.

"There's got to be another way!" said Eddie looking upwards.

"Afraid not," said Connie.

The time to get him to the top was excruciatingly painful. Connie concentrated on getting him to different levels, but Polly feared her heart would burst from beating so fast, as she constantly searched around for anyone that might spot them.

Once on the top, hopping and carrying seemed unbelievably quick as they hastened across the warren to Connie's secret hideaway.

Once he was lying on the floor of the little wooden hut, Polly left. "Never ask me for anything ever again, Connie Boyton!" she called over her shoulder as she strode away.

Connie shut the rickety door that didn't quite fill the frame and turned around to regard the gift the sea had given her.

"Edmond or Eddie?"

He smiled. "Eddie. And you? What should I call you? Are you a Constance or a Connie?"

"I prefer Connie."

She began tapping her foot. Joseph would be wondering where she was, and she didn't want to arouse his suspicion. "You know Smiley?" she asked him.

"We have unfortunately met before."

"So, you understand what has happened to your… to your…"

"Yes, I understand."

Connie kept glancing between the door and the man lying on the floor.

"You need to go, so go."

"It might be nighttime before I can come back. There's a bucket in the corner for you, but there's nothing here to eat or drink until I come back. Will you be alright?"

"I think there's a strong possibility that I'll sleep right through until you return. Don't come unless it's safe to do so." He laid back his head and closed his eyes, effectively dismissing her. She wanted to kick him! She huffed as she left, and shut the door none too gently. Eddie chuckled, then pain took all thought from his head and he moaned in agony.

Connie heard his moan as she walked away, she stopped and considered going back, but there was nothing she could do. He was in the hands of God now.

Chapter 6

THE ROOM WAS HEAVY with peat-smoke, its sluggish thickness permeated the room with little warmth, but just enough irritation to force tears into Connie's eyes. She'd had no sleep, her every bone ached and her eyelids kept trying to close. But she couldn't allow herself to doze, for she might not wake till morning, and who knew if Eddie would survive the night without nourishment and warmth.

Finally, Joseph returned from the tavern, he sang as he walked and she sighed in relief for his good mood. She offered him a weak smile when he came through the door. "I have supper ready for you, husband."

He looked at her, as he swayed. "Sometimes, wife, I think you good… good… for something."

She bit her lip for she had an idea where this was leading and she wanted none of it. She pulled out his chair from under the table. "Sit down Joseph; let me take your boots from you."

He wobbled and bumped into the table, but he made the chair without falling. After she had pulled the second boot off, his body slumped in the chair. "Why did God curse me with you?"

"I don't know, husband, but I'm sorry for it." Of course she meant that she was sorry she had ever married him, and sorrier still that he still breathed, but she bowed her head so he couldn't read her face.

"Come to the bed tonight."

"Yes, Joseph."

He got up and stumbled into the other room without touching his supper. She heard him crash on the bed and went to look in on him. He was spread-eagled face down and already snoring.

Suddenly, new energy flooded her veins and she spun around. She flew across the room, and after putting on her cape she pulled out a bundle she had prepared while waiting for Joseph's return. She closed the door quietly, and started running.

Eddie woke to the sound of Connie striking flint. "Who's there?" His words sounded painful and harsh.

"'Tis only I, Eddie Calstock, fear not!" Connie lit the wick, and the tiny oil lamp she had brought with her burst into a small yellow light. When her eyes had grown accustomed to it, she started unpacking her bundle on the small square table. "I have some food for you, but maybe you should drink first."

She went to his side and hunched down next to him. "Can you sit up, do you think?"

It took a while, but he pushed himself up so that he was sitting with his back to the wooden panels of the hut. She lifted a cup before him, which he grabbed with both hands and drank its contents.

He spluttered and coughed.

"Slowly," said Connie.

"I thought you were giving me water."

"It's safer to drink cider around here, people think the water from the springs bring them disease, so we stick to what we know."

"Did you bring more?"

"Yes, but would you drink it in one go when I don't know when I'll be able to return?"

"Surely you have a bit more for me? I feel I must die for lack of a drink?"

She fetched the flagon off the table and poured another half-cup full. This time he drank it slowly.

"How's your leg?"

"Trying to kill me, I think if the pain gets any worse I shall finish the job myself!"

"Foolish talk!"

"Have you seen my leg? I'm sorely wounded."

"I thought you were a pirate!"

"As I no longer have a ship, a crew or plunder, I think I can safely say my pirate days are over."

Connie took a slow look over his body. From his boots to the bandanna tied around his neck, every part of him was pirate, including his long, disorderly ringlets of hair.

"So, I may need a new outfit, but clothes don't maketh the man."

"No, but they do reveal his trade."

He shrugged. "True."

Connie went to the table and returned with some bread and cheese wrapped in a cloth. "I will fetch you some warm pottage tomorrow morning after Joseph has gone out in the boat."

He accepted the food. "Thank you," he said and took a large bite of the bread. While Eddie munched on his food, Connie removed the cloth wrapped around his leg. He hissed in pain.

"Sorry," she said, "but I must clean it or sickness will take you."

He nodded and braced himself as she lifted the last piece. His chest rose and fell in rapid succession, and a sweat broke out on his forehead. Leaving the cloth under his leg to catch the spill, she poured some rum over the laceration which was an angry red.

Eddie clenched his fists and bit his lip, but he didn't cry out. Connie only had a small amount of rum, so she poured it slowly ensuring the whole wound was drenched. When that was done, she opened a small pot containing honey and began to smear it over the cut with her fingers. He jumped several times and sighed in relief when she took a clean cloth and began to wrap it around his calf. His eyes were smarting, but he lifted his chin in order for the tears to recede.

He studied her as she cleared away the dirty cloth and put the lamp to the side of him. "Did you find anything attached to my body when you found me?"

She looked surprised. "Like what?"

He examined her for a moment, and shook his head, "Never mind."

"I have to go, but I'll return tomorrow as soon as I can. Don't fall asleep with the lamp on for I have no spare oil to fill it, and although its flicker is faint, we also don't want any passerby to see it. They would surely come to investigate for no one lives hereabouts."

"Thank you kindly for your help, I appreciate that you've saved my life. I'm in your debt."

She shook her head. "It is nothing."

As Connie's hand reached for the door, he asked her, "Did any survive besides me?"

She froze before she answered and gave him the dreadful news, "None." Then she left, afraid to talk about the devilish deaths that had befallen those who had managed to swim to shore.

A few hours later, the sun broke over the horizon as Connie stood and searched for pilchards. Joseph should have been there, but she'd known there'd be no waking him after the amount he must have drunk last evening. So, she had waded through the turning tide, and reached the island not long after she had left the shepherd's hut. Although she'd carried her boots, and held her skirt and underskirts as high as she could, she'd still got wet. Cold and uncomfortable she had hardly slept in the huer's lookout hut.

For appearance's sake, she knew the fishermen would have risen early as normal, with the exception of her husband, to maintain the resemblance of normality. They'd be assembled now along the quay, repairing nets and getting the boats ready to slip into the sea should the huer's cry reach them. She alternated between standing and sitting, and as the sun came to fullness the pilchards had still not come.

Hearing the crunch of feet, Connie spun around, half fearing that Smiley approached. She breathed easy when she saw it was only Polly.

The pirate came and sat next to her. "Does he live?"

"He does."

"No fever?"

"Not yet at least."

They sat in silence for a little while, and Polly joined Connie in searching for the shoals.

When Polly broke the silence, her words were heavy. "Do not fall for his handsome face, lassie. He is not the man to rescue you from your misery."

"Tsk! Who do you take me for? I don't desire a man, any man let alone a pirate! No matter how fair of face… or rather dashing!"

Polly turned her body to face her friend. "The sloop that brought him here belonged to Hawk-Eye or Captain Harry Hawkins for his true name." Connie turned to face her. "Do you know that name, Connie?"

"I know a little."

"Do you know that he and his crew are the… were the… most ruthless of all pirates?"

"I have listened to some gruesome tales."

"It's said that Earnest Eddie is the real mastermind behind their missions. It was Hawk-Eye's ship, therefore he was captain, but really it was Eddie who ruled the nest of vipers."

Connie gulped and stood up, pretending to search for pilchards to hide her discomfort.

Polly stood as well. "Whatever you're thinking, I beg you… don't run away with him. You're too soft a person to live the kind of life he would lead you into."

"I am not soft!"

"You think because you've received a beating or two that you're hardened, but I have watched you Connie Boyton, and you cut deep and care much. Pretend to the world if you must that you don't care for anything, but I know you. And I'm telling you, Edmond Calstock is nothing but bad news."

Connie's shoulders dropped as the fight suddenly left her. "I'm so tired," she sighed, and she meant from more than a lack of sleep. Looking back up again, she asked, "Would you be able to sneak me a blanket? I have but one thin one that Joseph wouldn't notice had gone missing. He really needs another."

"I can get you two warm ones. They are in my trunk; no one will miss them but me. I will take them to him when I am able."

"Thank you. I'll get them back to you as soon as he's gone."

Polly then acted out of character. She grabbed Connie in her arms and hugged her tight. The comfort of it brought tears to Connie's eyes. "I should go before Smiley rises," said Polly. "But I must ask you first… did you find anything on the beach when you found Eddie?"

"No. Why do you ask?"

Polly considered how much she should say; eventually, she took off her hat and scratched her chin with it. "There is a rumor that he stole the Rosalie's pirates' chest, Smiley has put a bounty on his head and offered a larger share of the gold to the pirate who finds it. They are all of them lusting for riches now. The rum and leather no longer booty enough for them. If they find him... and whoever helps him... they will be quick to kill. I thought that if maybe you had found the treasure, you could hand it over and they'd not be interested in him anymore, or the person helping him." The whole time she talked she pierced Connie with a glance that demanded truth and understanding of what she had told her. She hoped that Connie wouldn't guess her lie, for indeed Smiley would still want Eddie dead even if he had the gold, for dead men tell no tales as he was fond of repeating. But she had hoped it would take the heat out of the situation and give Eddie a chance to run before they found him, therefore leaving Connie safe.

"I didn't find it Polly; if I had I would truly give it to you to save his life, and ours. You saw, he had nothing on his person except the gold medallion around his neck."

Polly took a deep breath and let out a massive sigh. "I'd hoped you had, it would have saved you both. Look!"

Connie turned and looked out to sea; there was a massive discoloration in the water. She grinned, cupped her hands to her mouth and yelled across the island, "Here-by, here-by." It was too late in the day to swing a lamp.

Polly cupped her hands, and with a wink at Connie also shouted out, in a much louder voice than Connie could muster, "Here-by, here-by."

Joseph would have throttled her if she hadn't returned to tell him the fish had come. Maybe her calls had echoed this far, for he was already heading to the beach and so their paths crossed.

"You were the lookout?"

"Yes, Joseph."

He nodded and hurried on towards the beach before he missed the boats and his share of the catch payment.

Connie suddenly had a thought and chased after him. "Husband?"

His response was a grunt.

"Between the night's activities and the lookout I haven't slept. Would it be acceptable to you if I didn't come to the beach to help with packing the pilchards?"

He was about to burst an angry retort when he noticed her face. An angry red gash peeped out from under her hair on her forehead. Huge black bags lay under her eyes, her cheeks looked unnaturally drawn and it was obvious she was on her last legs. No doubt the villagers would look at him as the cause. "Very well."

She could have kissed him she was so relieved, well not really! Nevertheless, as she walked away, the thought of kissing took a firm hold in her mind. However, it was not to her husband that her thoughts did wander.

Once home she did her routine chores and when completed sat on the stool exhausted. She would wait until the pottage was done, and then go and visit her fugitive. Tiredness stole her away into sleep. She dreamt of shipwrecks and a handsome pirate who stole her heart.

She woke with a start. It was already late in the afternoon. Joseph had not returned which meant he'd gone straight to the tavern again. She needed to get to Eddie and back again before he returned.

Fear sped her heartbeat to deep thuds, yet excitement danced around the edge of it. Reckless! She had never been that in her life! There was no holding back the smile at the edge of her lips as she raced back to the shepherd's hut.

"Don't be gone." Her body prickled with dread that he might have left. Why she should still want him to be there she didn't know. But she did. New purpose to her day encouraged her to rush to his side with unladylike haste.

She owned three dresses, all she had worn since marrying Joseph. Two work dresses and one for best, and that one not worn for three years past as she no longer went to church on Sundays. Today after her chores, she had slipped on and tied up the laces of the one she had previously loved the best. The deep red of its petticoat had long ago washed out to a pale insipid pink, an exact reflection of her life she had thought with some amusement.

As she raced across the warren, Connie recalled her past. Her parents had been partners, working their way through each day together. Rarely an argument had passed between them, but neither had tender words towards each other she realized. Was that the best that anyone could wish for in life – a comfortable companion? Yet, Mrs. Tucker, the smithy's wife, was constantly looking at her husband with love-filled doe-eyes, and constantly giggled when he went near her. Was that real love? A deep sigh caused her chest to rise and fall, what did it matter? Whatever love was, it was never coming her way.

Hesitating outside the shack door, she wondered what she would find inside. Would he still be there? Might he have died while she slept? The door creaked as she pushed it open. He was still there, lying on the floor and in obvious pain. His eyes flicked open as she came in, but besides that he didn't move.

"I've fetched you some pottage, can you sit?"

He moaned as he pushed himself up. His entire body was now aching and not all of it from his injuries. The floor was cold and hard and he longed for his hammock. The battering the sea had given him had left his body covered in bruises; it was fair to say not a part of him didn't ache.

She had carried the bowl in her hands with a plate on the top to try to keep it warm, but it was only lukewarm when he ate it. Still, he wolfed it down. It was a good sign that he was hungry and Connie was sure he'd gotten lucky and would recover well.

He leaned back against the wall as she re-dressed his leg, after smearing more honey on it. It still looked angry, but already the skin was showing signs of knitting together.

"The blanket is thin I'm afraid, but it's all I can sneak out of the house without Joseph noticing."

He pulled it around him, up to his neck and peeked at her from over the edge. During the time since she'd left him, he had swung between fever hot and freezing cold. He was more grateful for the covering than he could tell her.

"Is your husband a brute?"

"What? Why do you ask that?"

Eddie grabbed her arm and pushed up her sleeve. Bruises at various stages of healing marked her arm. She snatched back her arm and hastily pulled down her sleeve.

"That's none of your business."

"I can't abide a man who hits a woman, cowards all of them!"

She sat back on her haunches and studied him, "Says the man with the reputation of a blood-thirsty pirate!"

He laid his head back against the wood and closed his eyes. "If I survive this, I will share my life story with you, maybe then you will judge me less."

She had no answer. After a brief moment, the food and the needed warmth had their affect and Eddie fell asleep. She studied him, taking in every curve and shape of his fine face. His mouth had fallen slightly open, and his teeth gleamed healthy white against his weather-beaten bronzed skin. Oh Lord, but he really was the most attractive man she had ever set eyes upon!

Glad that he had gone to sleep, and her visit could be short, Connie hastened home before Joseph knew of her absence.

Chapter 7

WIND WHISTLING THROUGH THE GRASSES created eerie echoes that attacked Eddie's senses. It infiltrated his unsettled sleep with nightmares, and Eddie tossed and turned as he fought his night demons. One of which was a man whose eyes had pleaded for mercy as Eddie's sword had run him through. 'No mercy' Hawkins had warned them, and so no mercy he had shown. As a sheep follows without question, Eddie had been sucked into the life of a pirate, learning how to kill without much thought and no regrets. He'd been forging his place in the world, carving out his path and climbing to the top, which he had done more quickly than any before him. His quick-thinking and strategy-forming mind had given him a reputation for being the brains behind all their raids. No one knew but himself and Hawkins that the captain had caught Eddie stealing from the crew's hoard. Such a deed should have resulted in walking the plank and a sea death, for to break the Pirates' Code was an unthinkable betrayal. Eddie had wanted a future as a man of means living in London in the finest of styles. His greed and determination to be rid of the pirate's life had almost brought about his demise. Once indebted to the captain, his life had become even more intolerable, as Hawkins pushed them into bloodier and bloodier battles.

He awoke drenched with perspiration. What damnation this enforced confinement had become. It left him alone to ponder his memories and he liked it not at all!

When Connie entered the hut, his eyes appeared crazed from a tormented night, and his temper was high. He swore a pile of verbal abuse towards her, cursing and blaming her for his miserable existence. Name-calling and shouts had long ago lost their power over Connie, and she set about cleaning his wounds as if he'd greeted her with a cheery disposition.

Today he would not be still, knocking her away with flapping arms, and cursing with words that made her blush. At first anger had made her pulse beat faster, but before she had built up a fire to retaliate, he started sobbing. His body wracked with the pain of body and soul. Her heart went out to him and for his torment. She could not get him to eat anything, and had to console herself with the fact that at least he'd drunk some cider. She stayed with him as long as she could, but in the end, she had to leave him alone with his terrors.

Polly came later that night, when she was sure no one would follow her. By the time she arrived at the hideaway, Eddie's fever had broken and he lay shivering on the floor. She knelt beside him and covered him with the two blankets she had sneaked out of the inn. His eyes flew open as she put her hand on his forehead to try to gauge the fever"

"Who are you?" he said huskily, for his throat was dry and sore.

"I'm the person who has brought you blankets and a bottle of rum."

"Do I know you?"

"You don't remember? I helped to bring you here from the beach."

"Yes, I remember now, there were two of you. My thanks are yours."

"I'm not here because of you and need not your thanks. I'm here only to help you get well enough to leave, before you get poor Connie murdered."

"Her husband?"

"Umm, yes I think he'd try to kill her if he found out about you. But it's Smiley that you both need to worry about."

Eddie pushed himself up. "He knows I live?"

"Not for sure, but the lack of your lifeless body gives him cause to believe you still live. They've been searching the coastline for signs of you."

Eddie leaned forward slightly. "And are there any signs to find?"

"A worn footpath is forming in the fields that lead straight to your door. If you see Connie before I do, you need to tell her to vary her way here. Better still, be a kind man and tell her never to return! Her life is already tainted with sadness; I wish no more of it for her."

"I'll do that. I owe her my life. I'll not put hers in danger any more than it is already."

"I hope you're a man of your word." Polly stood up, getting ready to leave.

"Why does she not leave the man if he beats her so?"

Polly squinted at Eddie and placed her hands on her hips to emphasize her displeasure. "Don't you be thinking the maid is weak or submissive, she is a survivor who maneuvers through life looking for the least stress and pain possible in her dark world. Joseph may batter her body, but by God, her spirit is as strong as the ocean!"

"And no one stands for her?"

Polly colored slightly. "Would that my lot in life be different, I would stand for her, but alas she has no kin to defend her."

"And the villagers?"

"Mind their own business."

"As does most of the world. Poor lass."

"I'm telling you," Polly wagged her finger at him, "you mustn't let slip that you pity her, for she'll walk away from you and never return. That lassie doesn't have much, but pride and dignity she has in buckets full!"

"I'll mark your words and keep my thoughts to myself," said Eddie. "Yet more I'll do, I'll tell her I'm leaving and tell her not to return."

She thought he didn't notice anything, but Joseph paid attention to everything. "Where's the second blanket from your bed?" he demanded.

"I spilled something on it by accident, husband. I lifted it to take it to the stream for washing, but I caught the edge of it on the fire and before I knew it, it was ruined. I didn't want to concern you with it. I will sleep with one blanket and will not complain."

The rush and flow of her words raised his suspicions. Women were naught but clacking hens, all flashy feathers and worth no more than the eggs they hatched. He turned to Connie, his eyes deadly dark. His stupid wife couldn't even do that!

Connie couldn't help herself and she cowered, shrinking inwards as if to make herself invisible to the beating she knew was coming. Then she remembered the rum she had stashed away for such an occasion as this. It would be an appeasement that would hopefully soften his mood and deter the blow.

"I have something for you," she blurted out before dashing outside to fetch the bottle.

As she ran back into the house, she realized her mistake.

"Why did you hide it?" His words were like daggers in her chest.

"I was keeping it for a special day, for you Joseph." She moved to the table and put the bottle down so as not to drop it when his fists flew.

He punched her in the stomach, but it was as if his will wasn't in it. It was half-hearted, a kind of habitual thing that needed to be done, but today he could hardly be bothered with it.

He sat down and placed his elbow on the table. He leaned into his hand, his head needing support from the alcohol-induced weakness. "When the power of drink takes me, I imagine I am king of my hearth, lord over my wife and master to many sons. When I wake, I'm forced to remember that my barren wife has given me no sons. If I was not such a God-fearing man, I would get rid of you and find me a proper wife." On the wall behind him, his shadow danced to the tune of the burning embers. Larger than life, the black image took on the appearance of an ogre ready to devour her. She remained curled in a ball on her makeshift bed in the corner and forced her mind to a place where Joseph didn't exist.

Long after his snores echoed through the house, Connie lay awake and wrestled with her emotions. Against Polly's advice, she mused over what it would be like to run away with Eddie. Was it possible to flee her marriage prison, and break for freedom with him? Would he really be able to protect her if Joseph hunted them down and found them? It was almost sunrise, when she finally allowed her mind to slow enough for sleep to come for her.

The next morning a headache tightened her brow and made her eyes long to remain closed. But she was a sturdy lass accustomed to pain, so she made her aching body move. Mind over matter her mother had always told her. Mind over matter.

Some thought her a mouse caught in a trap, but she knew better. She was a spider, if anything, running up and down her web of repetition, catching morsels to feed her husband, tame him, subdue him… until the day when she would be free. No mouse. No trap. No indeed!

Joseph glared at her as she shakily climbed out of bed and stood up. Jabbing a pointed finger at her with every word, he said, "I'm master of this house, and you'll do my bidding with no complaint. Do you understand?"

"Yes Joseph."

The first 'yes Joseph' that had fallen from her lips seven years earlier had been the first of thousands to follow. That first one had stuck in her throat and made her feel sick. Now, they slipped off her tongue with ease and no meaning.

For a moment, she wondered if he was going to strike her again, but he turned and made for the door. Once there he stopped and turned to look at her. "If I find out you're hiding anything else from me, there will be the devil to pay!" With that he left, slamming the door behind him. Her head rolled as the sound sent waves of pain through her.

"Beast!" she hissed and sat down on the stool delicately. Clutching her head in her hands she wondered how she could carry on like this. He was becoming increasingly violent and the beatings more frequent. As she looked into the cold fireplace and thought about the fire she needed to get started, she pondered on the likelihood that one day her husband would fulfill his constant threats and kill her. Maybe it was time to seek a new life after all?

A part of her didn't care if Joseph returned early and caught her on her mission to visit her pirate. It would bring an end to their marriage, one way or another, and for that she was growing quite desperate.

Eddie took one look at her and cursed. "The man deserves to hang!"

"No man has ever been hung for mistreating his wife."

"Well they ought to be!"

Connie couldn't help but smile, it felt intoxicating to have someone on her side. "I see you're much improved," she said.

"Which I wouldn't be, without you," he said with tenderness.

His words made her catch her breath. Then he ruined it.

"How do you not murder him in his sleep?"

That *look* could have sent him scurrying into the 'naughty corner' if he'd been at school.

"Other than not wanting to swing in the hangman's noose you mean?"

His shrug admitted the juvenile comment had not been serious.

"He loved me once," she said. "It was not his fault I stole his dreams and left him empty and bitter."

"And how, pray tell, did you do that?"

Connie sat on the floor beside him, crossed her legs and told her story. She reminisced about her happy childhood, and became sad when she recalled how her parents had died within weeks of each other from influenza.

"Two days after the funeral Joseph turned up in his Sunday best. He knew I was being evicted from the farm and came to offer me a solution to my homelessness."

"Marriage in exchange for a home."

"Yes. I knew of his temper of course, the whole village does. But I was sixteen and too frightened to consider any other options. My neighbors encouraged me, saying I could do far worse. He wasn't always handy with his fists. At first he treated me well enough, I couldn't complain. Then time slipped by and his displeasure at my empty womb began to grow. He took me completely by surprise the first time he hit me. When he failed to apologize the next day, I knew what my life was to become."

"You have no children?"

"No, I'm cursed don't you know! Barren as a dry desert and a shameful curse to my husband." Her words paled into silence as she couldn't help the pain that filtered through.

"You might have children yet, it ain't impossible. You're still young."

"Oh, I do not want them! I've seen how having children takes a woman in her youth and turns her into an aged hag, ever tired and run down. Oh no, that's not the life I'm going to have!"

"And what life is that?"

Connie aired her dreams aloud for the first time in her life. Escape from Bigbury-on-Sea and her vicious husband, find a place where no one would know her, and build her own farm, with apple trees too, lots of apple trees. She'd make her own cider and people would come from miles around to buy it. She had everything worked out. How much money she would need and the equipment she would have to buy, and what her home would look like.

"I'll admit," said Eddie when she had finished, "that is quite some dream. I hope that on this farm that you'll have guns to protect yourself?"

"I will indeed have a varied assortment of them!"

"You can shoot?"

"I have knowledge of guns and have fired one a few times when I was young. Joseph sold my father's pistol a long time back though."

"Maybe, he considered such a deadly weapon in your possession to be tempting fate too greatly?"

There was a pause as her startled eyes took in his meaning and the sparkle in his, and before she knew it, the two of them fell about laughing.

"I never considered that when he took it from me, how funny if that was indeed the truth of it and he feared me?"

Connie prepared to leave.

As much as Eddie realized he didn't want to, he had to discourage her from returning.

"You mustn't come back 'ere, at least not 'til I've left. Give me another day and then I'll be gone."

From laughing to disappointment before she'd even reached the door.

"There's only one man that tells me what to do, Eddie Calstock, and that's not you." With a disdainful glare she left.

Chapter 8

FOR THREE DAYS, THE FISH FAILED TO COME. Joseph, struggling from lack of drink, was in a mood so foul Connie grew scared, though she hid it well. Joseph had moped about the house all morning, but by late afternoon he kicked a stool over and declared he was going to the Sloop for a drink on the never-never. Connie rolled her eyes, for this meant when the fish did come again, he would have already spent his wages on drink. Still, it took him away from her and for that she was grateful.

With Joseph gone, Connie was able to go to Eddie without worrying. She packed up a cloth with a bit of food, wrapped her shawl around her shoulders and set off across the warren. The wind whistled through the bracken, not biting but fresh and revitalizing. If she hadn't been so tired, she would have slowed her pace and enjoyed the smells coming off the land. Bluebell, cowslip and pink Campion waved at her through the deep greens of grass and the white fluffy heads of great water parsnips – it was a joyous sight that would normally have caused her to sing, but today her gaze fell only upon the earth where her next step must land. She was somewhat taken by surprise when Eddie's hideaway loomed before her.

As she raised her head, Eddie came into view. He was standing in the doorway, leaning on the door jamb. She picked up speed and raced towards him. "You shouldn't be standing, someone might see you! Get back inside!"

He smiled at her abrasive greeting, but complied and limped back inside. After dropping her shawl on the chair, she set to opening the cloth and displaying the food she had fetched.

"Not much I'm afraid, but it will sustain you."

"It's a feast, Connie Boyton, for which I'm truly grateful, although as I tell you every day – you shouldn't come."

This argument was getting old and so she chose to ignore it. One glance at him revealed the insincerity of his comment. "Won't you sit?" she asked him, while she herself sat on the floor not too far from the low burning fire.

He picked up some cheese and bread and then lowered himself down beside her on the floor. He broke the bread in half and passed a chunk to her. At first it looked like she would refuse, but when her stomach growled, she accepted. She was grateful when they ate in silence. There was no fight in her today and no strength to parry words like others handle swords. Soon, the lack of sleep, warm fire and bread took their toll… and her eyes closed. Eddie shifted slightly closer, put his arm around her shoulder and pulled her head tenderly towards his chest. A slight sigh escaped her lips and in the blink of an eye she was fast asleep.

Sometime later, when it was obvious she wouldn't wake; Eddie lifted her and placed her upon his bed of straw. He stoked the fire a little and then lay down beside her, wrapping his arms around her and pulling her body close to his to keep her warm. Maybe it was his touch and the safety it offered, but Connie slept like a baby and did not stir until early morning dreams created of floating dead pirates.

As soon as she opened her eyes she knew she was in trouble. She sprang up from the floor and stared down at Eddie, who was waking and beginning to sit up. She gave him a hefty kick in the shin before fleeing for home. He called her name but she kept running. Joseph was going to be furious, oh please God have mercy and let him not have returned.

Arriving at the farmhouse out of breath, she waited a moment before carefully inching open the door. When no sound met her, she sighed in relief, realizing he had once again had too much to drink and not returned.

She took off her cape and put it on the hook behind the door. Then she put on her apron and was just reaching for the broom when the door barged open. Her heart sank. His face was as black as thunder.

"Where have you been?"

"Nowhere."

He crossed the room in three strides and slapped her across the face.

"You've just come back, I saw you."

"I only went for an early walk, Joseph, that's all."

He twisted her arm behind her back and marched her into the bedchamber. She bit her lip until it bled, but she did not cry out. He threw her on the bed and stepped away to take off his clothes. She didn't move; a frozen porcelain doll. When he turned back with his belt in his hand, his nightshirt danced around his body, laughing, mocking the overweight man he had become. Once he had been a towering hulk, now he was a blundering giant, heavy and slow. She could run out of the room before he reached her –

that would be easily done. But she had learned that the least resistance resulted in the quickest healing, so she didn't move, not a muscle.

It seemed that for a moment his vision cleared and he saw her. He stopped dead and glared at her. She could see anger building, taking on new heights, and though she didn't move, her heart quickened and her chest rose and fell in rapid succession without her permission.

"Everyone thinks you are the walking dead, with your expressionless face and few words. But *I* see behind those eyes. *I* know you have a scheming brain, but be warned... you'll never be free of me wife, not as long as I live!"

Her thought was instant... Let's hope you die soon then. Joseph caught the glimmer of that thought behind her dull eyes. He barked a laugh, amused, fully understanding her not so well-hidden hatred of him.

"Go on... let it out my girl, for good God I would prefer a wife who stood up for herself!"

Her muscles instantly slackened, her heart rhythm forced into submission slowed and stilled her rising chest. Unresponsive, offering no challenge, she would never, never, give him what he wanted!

Accustomed as she was to the pitying glances of the villagers, she paid them scarce attention normally. Today, however, a cloud of gloom hung low over her head. Her body was used to physical pain and her mind accustomed to being numb. However, the glimmer of hope that Eddie presented had pierced her wall of indifference and now pain was seeping from her heart like a slow-flowing leak.

Mrs. Margaret Neale, the vicar's wife, took one look at Connie's bruised and forlorn face and the stoop of her shoulders, and took it upon herself to comfort the poor fisherman's wife. "You must come in for a drink of warm cider my dear. It has been so long since I've seen you in church and we worry about you so." The kindly woman would not take no for an answer, and Connie got swept along by her warm enthusiasm, and a sudden longing for a word or two of feminine comfort. She could not pour out her woes to this woman, but she could bask in her comfort for a short while.

"John!" bellowed Mrs. Neale as they entered the vicarage. "John, we have a visitor."

"We do?" responded the deep, mellow voice of the vicar, before he appeared to join them in the hallway. "Well-well, if it isn't Constance Wakeham, what a pleasure, pure delight. Come on in, come on, and let us get reacquainted."

"Now dear, as you married them, you know very well she's been Constance Boyton, for these seven years past," said Mrs. Neale swinging off her short cape and placing in on the stand.

"Connie," said Connie quietly. "It has been a long time since anyone called me Constance."

"Why ever not? Constance is such a beautiful name, is it not my dear?" the vicar said while nodding over zealously at his wife. "And as for Wakeham, well that's what I christened you, so it has kind of stuck." He smiled at Connie, the creases around his eyes somehow revealing the warmth in his words.

"Connie is perfectly fine, dear," his wife replied throwing Connie a quick wink.

Connie couldn't help but smile. For a long time she had not thought about the vicar and his wife, but now returned to their company she was compelled to remember how well she liked them.

The vicar of Bigbury was a thin and earnest man, his wife a buxom woman with a round, rosy-apple face and sparkling eyes. By appearance it seemed they were the height of opposition, yet their spirits mingled together as one and the love betwixt them shone for all to see.

"Sit by the fire, my dear," urged Mrs. Neale, "I will fetch us some warmed cider, and my husband here will bore you with tales of no significance." All three of them laughed as she left the room.

Connie perched herself carefully on the very edge of a seat near the fire, very conscious of the fact that her skirts were far too dirty for this dainty drawing-room. She folded her hands in her lap and chewed her lower lip. The vicar sat in the chair opposite and studied her with serious intent. His brow creased and his eyes scrunched. Without his Sunday black cassock she was reminded that he was, after all, just a man. It made her feel uncomfortable, and she wondered why on earth she had allowed his wife to usher her here.

As if sensing her thoughts, the vicar leaned forward in his chair to better portray his sincerity. "Is there something you would like to discuss with me child?"

She shook her head, and the vicar sat back obviously disappointed. His expression carried his every thought, and Connie was sure he must be glad his thoughts were always so attentive and caring towards his parishioners. He twitched his thin hawked nose, and she remembered the jester from her childhood, it meant he was displeased. Her shoulders sank, it didn't matter how kindhearted these people were... there was nothing they could do for her.

Mrs. Neale soon returned with pewters of warm cider and a plate of flat breads flavored with rosemary. She smiled softly towards Connie as she handed her the drink. This woman was the epitome of a vicar's wife and oozed generosity, Connie knew that not one person in the whole of Devonshire would find her disagreeable.

They sat, the three of them, for a short while making small talk. Eventually, it seemed Mrs. Neale could hold her tongue no longer. "You must tell us Connie, if you are in danger, for we have heard worrying things about..." (For a dreaded moment, Connie thought she was going to say something about Eddie.) ..."your husband's temper."

Connie blushed and surprised herself, for she had believed she was beyond such embarrassment these days. So used was she to her bruises that it surprised her that other people still spotted them.

Being good was not sufficient, she thought as she looked at their kindly faces. So she hung back from confessing her woes, knowing they could not interfere between a man and his wife, no matter how much they would like to. She warmed her hands around the pewter and gazed upon the apple liquid. Apples were one of her favorite things in life, and she had planted seeds wherever she could when she was young. Her fingers were green, people had acknowledged, as her trees grew and bore much fruit. Though not one had grown on the warren around her husband's home, and she'd been forced to sneak across the land of her childhood and become a scrumper. She fancied the folk who had moved into her old farm knew she stole the apples, but they never did anything about it.

She wondered what she could say to these kind people before her, she could hardly lie, as the bruises on her face were clear to see, she was only thankful they could not see her arms and legs.

"Do you know the sacred prayer, child?" asked the vicar.

"I do."

"And do you say it often?"

Connie looked him in the eye, she would not lie. "No."

Mrs. Neale grimaced. "Only the dear Lord can help us in our hour of need," she gushed, trying to cover up her reaction.

"And how many times should you pray without an answer before you must succumb to the fact that God has no interest in you and your life?"

"The Lord is interested in all our lives," said the vicar inching forward in his seat, preparing for the sermon that was building in his heart. Mrs. Neale placed a gentle hand upon his knee. He settled back in his seat, his wife had such wisdom and he bowed to it now, as he was so oft to do.

Connie thought about the field behind the church where fishermen and their families slept under simple markers, waiting for the second-coming and their longed for better, eternal life. What a sweet hope that must be, and for a moment she envied them their faith. But it was not for her. She could not believe in that which every other soul did, for if she did she would have to believe that she truly was cursed and had been rejected by God. The hand of self-pity gripped her chest and she winced in pain.

"Oh child," gushed Mrs. Neale who flew from her chair and knelt at Connie's feet. "We know what a monster he is, we truly do. Would that we could rescue you... why not? Let us steal you away in the night and send you to safety someplace he will never find you."

"Margaret!" the admonishing tone of her husband made her spin on her knees to look at him. "You cannot say such things; whatever would people say if we came between a man and his wife?" he snapped at her.

"And what will God say if we do not?"

The vicar got up from his chair and began to pace.

"Do not fret yourself Vicar Neale, I'm not asking for your help. Indeed, I'm only here right now at the insistence of your good wife. I'll be on my way, have not a fear."

"No, no!" Mrs. Neale placed her hands on Connie's knees to prevent her from rising. "We must help her, John!"

John stopped his pacing and came to stand beside them. "What would you have us do, child?"

She wanted to say nothing, but from somewhere in her past a need for blessing arose. "Please pray for me."

"Oh dear child, we can surely do that."

John Neale knelt beside his wife. The two of them clenched their hands together in front of them in the common way. "Dear

Lord," began the vicar, but after that his words became a blur to Connie and she heeded them not. After some time which was impossible to measure, Connie instinctively knew the vicar had emptied his heart and was drawing to a close.

"We ask thee oh Lord, to bless thy servant Joseph, to forgive him his trespasses and have mercy on his soul..."

"Forgive him!" blurted Connie before John could complete his Amens. "Forgive him for beating me black and blue?" The vicar's last words had pulled her from the place of musing where she had wanted to be drenched in blessings and comforted by soft words. She jumped out of her seat, startling the couple who still knelt.

"Why could you not ask God to bless me?! To bless my womb and bless me with a child? Maybe then my brute of a husband would mellow in his despise of me and beat me less!"

"Oh, Connie, Connie," wailed Margaret in much distress. "Child, we pray that for you nearly every day. We thought only if God would mend Joseph's ways as well, you might have a chance at a happy union."

Connie crumbled like sand through fingers and slumped once more into her seat. "I am sorry for my outburst," she said softly, "you must think me truly wicked."

"No, we do not," said the vicar placing a hand upon her head. "We think you harshly done by, and *that* is the truth."

Margaret grasped hold of Connie's hands in hers, and with imploring eyes sought Connie's attention. "We believe that forgiveness is a very powerful thing. Both in giving and receiving, but mainly in giving. I know, I really do, that to ask you to forgive the man who beats you is a thing that will probably seem impossible, but with God all things are possible, and who knows what might come if you are able to do this Godly thing."

Chapter 9

WHEN THE TIDE WAS HIGH and Burr Island inaccessible from the mainland, Smiley took Bill Bones and Snake-Eye and set off for the lean-to behind the inn. Inside the bitty makeshift covering was Captain Harry Hawkins, tied, gagged and bound to a chair.

Only Smiley's crew knew he was there, as far as the villagers understood all the crew of the Rosalie were dead.

Snake-Eye took the gag off Hawkins.

"You're a dead man, Smiley. When others find out what you've done to one of your own they'll come for your blood and you'll dance with Jack Ketch!"

Smiley flicked his eyes towards Snake-Eye, who immediately punched Hawkins in the face. His head rolled back and blood streamed from his cut lip.

"Tell me where you offloaded your treasure and I'll let you live."

"I've told you every day… the only treasure we had, was in a chest that Eddie Calstock stole in our desperate hour." He turned his head and spat blood on the floor. "Curse the man!"

Smiley folded his arms and leant against the wall. Bill Bones threw a punch at the bound captain, this time into his stomach. Hawkins doubled and retched, but nothing came forth as he had been without food for several days. "Just kill me. What pirate-honor have you that you would let me die slowly from starvation? It is not the way of us sea kings. Give me the plank or set me free!"

"One of your men, what was his name again...?" Smiley looked at Bill Bones.

"Fontana."

"Arr that's right, the short man with the profound hand gestures; who wouldn't keep them still until we tied him up. And whose tongue would not cease his incessant foreign jabber until we threatened to cut it out." Smiley turned his gaze back to Hawkins. "Well, Fontana, memorable fellow that he was, told us you stopped at several islands in the Caribbean. He said only you and your boatswain, what his name..."

"Earnest Eddie," said Snake-Eye.

"Yes, that's him. Well, apparently the two of you were as thick as thieves and would take no other with you when you rowed to shore. So if you weren't looking for a place to hide your booty what were you doing?"

"We were looking for a new place to live, with the Bahamas and Nassau being lost to us years ago it has been hard to find a place to settle. You know that Smiley, that's why you're here, hiding away on this pee-wee piece of rock."

Snake-Eye punched him again. This time so hard it took a while for Hawkins to become fully focused again. When he did manage to look up, Smiley could tell he was done for the day; his eyes had become glazed and unseeing.

"You did for him too bad, Snake," said Smiley, rolling Hawkins head by the chin. We'll come back for him in the morning."

"He'll probably be dead by sunrise, Cap'n," said Bill Bones.

"What will be, will be. He's not going to tell us anything, no matter what we do, and that Fontana fellow might have been making it up about a treasure map to save his neck."

As the three men came out and shut the door, they failed to notice a slight movement beyond the shed.

The next morning the pirates continued their search for Edmond Calstock. Some went along the coast, and for the first time, some went inland. They decided to follow the River Avon, thinking maybe he had somehow passed them and made his way up the river to cover his tracks.

"Aren't you going with them today?" asked Polly, watching Smiley put on his finest clobber. The clothes he had set aside for when he could mix once more in polite society, the day that Polly truly believed would never come.

"No. I have a meeting with someone who will take the goods inland. We have to shift the loot before we are found out; the village grows more hostile by the day."

"Will you be long?"

He turned to her and glared. "You're asking a mighty bunch of questions today."

"It's just I would like to visit with Connie. She has said she will teach me how to stuff a rabbit for a fine roast, I thought to surprise you when I display my new hidden talents!"

She struck a pose like a man wide-legged and hands on hips, and Smiley burst out laughing. "You, cook? That'll be the day. To answer your question it will depend how promptly he arrives in Bridge End and how quickly we can conclude business." Smiley put his hat on and nodded at her before leaving.

Polly sank onto a chair. She would wait awhile to be sure he had really gone, and then she would set about her dangerous plan.

Chapter 10

TODAY JOSEPH HAD REACHED A NEW LEVEL. He had kicked her numerous times in the stomach as she tried to protect herself on the floor. It was a first, and somehow she determined it would be the last time.

"What are you squawking about woman? Get a grip; do you want me to give you something proper to cry about?"

With tremendous effort and self-control, she forced a smile. "I'm sorry, Joseph. Let me take off your boots and then I'll fetch your supper." These things were dutifully done, and all the while her wifely servitude hid her hatred and resentment, though she cursed her hands for shaking so much. These things were necessary to prevent the rise of any suspicions, but as soon as she was on her own, she marveled at her skill of deception and thought the stage would suit her well, for surely there were no actors more accomplished at acting than her!

Eddie was standing in the doorway as Connie neared the hut. Unbeknown to her, he had watched her slow approach with growing anger.

"What's that sinner done now?" he hissed.

"I don't want to talk about it."

Eddie held the door open and she went inside and sat down tentatively on the only chair.

Each day she had come, a burning desire had flamed within him.

"I still have a limp, but I'm ready to leave. Come with me."

She laughed.

"I'm serious. Come with me and you'll be free of him."

"And where would I go, and what would I do, pray tell?"

"You 'ave choices, my girl, come with me and be my partner, and if that pleases you not, then I'll take you to a town of your choice. In towns there's always work to be found. You can start again, a new life. Start building your dream."

Connie's forehead puckered into a frown. "You're one of those adventurers, are you not? Rushing forward with eager spirit straight into trouble at every turn. Why, I believe even if you sat quietly minding your business, trouble would jump up to greet you. Should I yoke myself to such a fellow? I think not!"

"I'll admit, strife and I have been close companions over the years, but I'll be honest with you when I say… it's not the life I sought. I wanted a comfortable life, I'll not lie, who doesn't? But piracy was never my ambition. There's a dream within my heart that stretches and moans and longs to give birth. I want a corner of the world where I can raise my sons to 'ave a better chance in life than I ever did. A place where they will prosper and grow and find comfort."

His words brought confusion to her heart and mind. On one part it was the dream she wanted herself, and his words shone a light upon his character that had previously been missing. On the other hand, her distress was high, for she would never be the one to help him fulfill his dream.

"I'm cursed by God and barren!" After blurting the words, she lowered her head in shame.

Eddie reached forward and tipped her face back up by pushing her chin with a finger. When her downcast eyes finally looked up, he spoke.

"I was an orphan. I 'ave wondered often what my life would 'ave been if some kind couple had removed me from the degrading poorhouse. Children need love, even if they don't come from your womb. I would like ten little Calstocks' myself, and what of you, how many children will you raise?"

Connie laughed. Her being was flooded by a joy so pure it seemed to have come from Heaven itself. "Twelve," she declared. "We should have at least twelve!"

Laughter from his belly filled the squalid hovel that had become his temporary home. His thoughts spun on a wheel of repetition – we, she said *we*. As the laughter mellowed and his shaking shoulders stilled, he marveled at the beauty of the woman before him. Most of the time she appeared comely but no more than average, however, when smiling her face lit up and her eyes sparkled and there came upon her a radiance that quite took his breath away.

"That's settled, you'll come with me to a poorhouse and we'll bring salvation to twelve poor souls, shall we not?"

Connie nodded.

Eddie's face grew slightly somber. "Orphans are dying for lack of affection. There'd be fewer outlaws on the roads if people would open their hearts and doors to the plight of the motherless ones."

The truth of his words stung, for she knew he was right. Shame washed over her for never considering their plight. Not that she would ever contemplate bringing an innocent child into the household of Joseph Boyton – some things were worse than being parentless.

They looked at each with new eyes. Something had transpired between them, which meant that somehow they had just agreed their lives were linked together. Neither really knew what that might entail, but both suddenly yearned for a future that held within it something more promising than today.

Then, as it surely must, the moment passed and sensibility descended on them. They sat back from each other, only realizing now that they had leaned within inches of each other.

"I'm sure a place such as York, will be comfortable for you. I could travel with you there and see you settled before I move on."

He had dismissed her again. She bristled.

"I'm better off where I am. Better the devil you know, don't they say!"

"Don't be a fool. This is no place for you!"

"I'm no fool, Edmond Calstock!" She got up from the chair and rushed out before he could delay her. He moved to the doorway and watched her race away.

"You're a fool, Connie Boyton, for there's nothing in Bigbury-on-Sea for you but trouble!"

It was impossible to love someone in such a short time, this she told herself repeatedly. Yet, she could not take his face from her mind, nor the longing for his touch coming from her heart. Sleep was nearly impossible, and she woke the next day with heavy body and clumsy mind.

The day crept along at a snail's pace. She wouldn't allow herself to visit him today; too many emotions ran raw inside her. She felt confused. Both wanting him to love her and hating him at the same time. "Well not hating him," she mused, "his lifestyle, his choices, those are things I hate. How could I love him? It is impossible. I am being ridiculous, for no one can love a man before even a week has gone by!"

Loneliness and the lack of affection drive a hole in a person, so when the possibility of love presents itself, it becomes almost unbearable. So, despite her confused thoughts Connie took herself back to the shepherd's hut.

"I've brought you some food for your journey," she said, throwing down a cloth full of as much as she could hide from Joseph. "It's not much, but will see you on your way."

"So, you're eager for me to be gone?"

"It's not safe for you here."

"Arr, so you care for my wellbeing that's why you're casting me aside."

"I'm *not* casting you aside, you ridiculous man!"

"Then come with me, Connie. I've had time to think since our last conversation. I think I was hasty in my suggestion of York. I think it would be best if you came with me. On my travels I've heard many tales of the colonies and how a man may make his fortune there. Come with me to Liverpool, I will negotiate with a captain heading to the Americas that I'll work for nothing more than both our passage. We'll go and start building our dreams… together."

"The limits of my patience are well met, for only a fool would persist. I'm a married woman, and well you know it!"

"Many a woman has run away from a bad marriage before, you're naïve if you don't know that. On board ship I'll ask the captain to marry us, you shall land in America an honest woman, and none will know our story but you and me."

"Am I to run away with a pirate? How crazy must you think me!"

"I'm a pirate no more. For you, I'll become an honest man."

"Why?"

Eddie went quiet, before looking up at her with a half-smile. "Let us walk. I think I'll go insane for want of a variation to these dreadful walls."

She put the parcel down on the table and followed him outside. "We should head to the stream this way; it is not safe to venture towards the sea."

They walked a little way in silence. Connie had a longing to slip her hand in his, and clenched her hands together in irritation at the desire.

"My life hasn't turned out the way I planned. I seem to 'ave been burdened with great misfortune, unlucky you might say. The only lucky thing that ever happened to me was when a young, attractive, fisherman's wife dragged me from the sea and saved my life. Now, stuck in the hut, I have pondered on how much I owe this woman, and how much I would leave my dreams to chase hers simply that she may know my thanks."

"You irk me greatly. Yet somehow your words are speaking to my heart, and oh how it longs to surrender to you. But my head, oh Lord my head, it will not be quiet! If I find I must endeavor on the risky plank that would be my life if I walked with you, I must know every last detail about you. If I'm to align myself with you, then I insist on being knowledgeable in everything you've done. Be it good or bad, I will contemplate on all I hear, and when I'm ready I'll advise you of my decision. But, be warned Earnest Eddie Calstock... oh yes I see your dismay that I have learned of your true nature... if you lie to me I'll be gone. I will *not* return. And you may be left to your own will and devices."

His face was not so handsome when bitterness soured his mouth. With scrunched eyes, raised eyebrows, and a down-turned mouth he might be described as outright ugly! "Arr, your true colors do burst forth, as must all men's when given enough time."

Eddie's mouth moved as he grappled for the right words, eventually his look shot straight at her. They locked eyes, battling without words for dominance. He wanted it, she would not relent, the tilt of their chins evenly matched in stubbornness.

"Damn it woman! Why are you so bothersome?"

"I may answer that, if first you explain your arrogance."

His mouth dropped, "Woman, you are unbearable!"

"Then I'll leave you to your solace, you may look within the pools and ponder your magnificence but I'll not pander to your pride. Keep your secrets, for if you'll not share them, I'll not see you again."

With a flourish, she spun and made to leave.

"No, wait." Eddie grabbed her arm.

She flinched, instinct preparing her for a beating, her head dropped into her shoulders.

He let go of her immediately. "I'm sorry if I hurt you, but please don't go. I'll do as you ask and give you my life history."

Slowly, she turned her head and looked at him over her shoulder.

"All of it, I promise."

She searched his eyes and found only openness and truth.

"Very well, I'll tarry awhile as you regale me with your adventures, and what dastardly deeds you have committed, *Earnest Eddie*."

She had emphasized his name to remind him she already had knowledge of his past. There was nothing for it. He would be brutally honest and leave nothing out, if the chit decided to run for the hills by the time he had finished, well, that would be that, but she had asked.

"I was born in a poorhouse in London."

"You need not start at the very beginning. I did not ask for a chapter and verse account of your life!"

Eddie barked a laugh, and then indicated towards a fallen tree trunk they could use as a bench. "Sit with me. I'll gloss over my early years so as not to bore you, but if you want to know or even understand me, you should probably know where I come from."

She regarded the fallen tree trunk and wavered in her decision to hear what he had to say. What was the point of it? She had already decided she would not leave with him when he went. Yet, curiosity sat heavily in her spirit, and some unknown quarter of her being longed for him to reveal his secrets and so bind them together forever.

Connie sat on the trunk and Eddie sat beside her. He told her of the hardships afforded him in the orphanage and later. How he had sought an honest living as a seaman, and how Hawkins had commandeered the man-of-war he'd been apprenticed on. Hawkins had offered the young teenager the promise of riches and he had jumped at it. That day, Hawkins set the sailors of the ship loose in rowing boats to be saved by another ship. But later, he'd begun killing the sailors rather than letting them go. The change had come about slowly, and somehow insidiously worked itself amongst the crew until it became the common. It had put a mark upon all their heads, and if ever caught there was nothing but the gallows waiting for them. That constant knowledge that death was always close by banded them together like brothers and gave all of them a lust to gather their fortune and find a hidden place in the world to live.

"So you've killed your fair share of men?"

"I 'ave."

"And you think it's possible to change? I'm not so sure. It seems this buccaneer's life is upon your shoulders now, and you wear it well." Her thoughts lingered on just how *well* he portrayed a pirate. His tight curls framed his dashingly handsome face, and his broad shoulders stated strength. While his clothes (although a bit worse for wear) gave him that image of wildness and excitement. She found him altogether irresistible!

"I've decided to change, and I 'ave to believe it's possible. Without Hawk-Eye's blood-thirsty cry, I'm sure it's possible. Only believe in me my girl, and then I might believe in myself."

He reached over and took hold of her hand, raising it to his lips. She thought he was to kiss it; instead he laid his cheek upon it. "Dear Connie, please run away with me."

"I'll be honest and tell you I'm sorely tempted. But I don't think I have it in me to be a dishonest woman. I have a husband, and therefore my duty is to stay by his side."

"Damn duty I say!" He turned quickly and grabbed her face. He pulled her into him and smashed his lips against hers. She was too shocked to react. His mouth claimed hers and demanded a response. She gave in… only for a second before pulling away from him.

He went to say something, but she put her hand up to stop him from speaking. Without a word she turned and set off for Burr Island. She was in great need of seeing her friend.

Chapter 11

CONNIE WENT HOME FIRST to check the fire was stoked and the food cooked for her husband's return. Why she bothered she knew not. She was more than a little surprised to find Joseph had already returned and was snoring on the bed. His stale breath reeked of alcohol and fouled the whole house. Watching him sleep, Connie pondered on Eddie's words of the other day. If she was another type of woman, maybe she would have picked up the axe from the woodpile and swung it across his neck. Luckily for him she was not that kind of person.

"You have the strength of a horse and the brains of a flea, Joseph Boyton," mused Connie before going back into the kitchen. As she covered herself in her woolen cloak she chuckled. "Maybe I'm the one with the brains of a flea; after all I accepted the hand of a man well-known for his temper. What on earth had I been thinking? That my sweetness could mellow him? Stupid woman!" It seemed so laughable now, that she had once imagined that by a caring and tender approach she could ever have changed the person her husband was. That people do not change was a life-lesson learned too late.

Joseph was bound to give her a proper whipping if he woke and found her still not returned, but Connie was caught in a dream of escape and the devilment of adventure, and didn't care. She rushed along the coast towards the island, eager to talk with Polly and get her advice.

Alarm pricked her skin when she saw pirates searching the land along the river and realized it was time for Eddie to leave. Whether she would go with him, she still did not know.

Polly Fists was afraid. Although she knew Smiley loved her in his own way, she knew his capacity for anger was vast. What she had done was betray him, and if he learned of it, she feared her days were numbered. The tide was out as she approached Burr Island. She walked across the causeway trying to look nonchalant and put a little swagger in her stride. She needed to appear normal, though panic was hard to crush. She didn't know how she would be able to hide her jitters from Smiley. Her secret endeavors had taken much longer than she'd hoped. She feared when Smiley realized his prisoner was gone, and if he found out she had left the inn, he would come to the obvious conclusion. She felt sick as she climbed the slope to the inn and with her fingers crossed hoped against hope he'd not returned.

The door creaked as she opened it. She stood in the doorway waiting for a sound to alert her to the fact Smiley had heard it. When no sound came, she stepped in and tried to close the door as quietly as possible. Just as she was turning around, a sound turned her blood to ice.

The striking of flint against steel filled the dark shuttered room, and Polly lifted her head to see the sparks ignite a char cloth. She watched as it floated a moment, and then the oil lamp wick came to life. A shadow leaned forward and blew on it gently until the flame took and the lamp came to life.

"It seems you let the fire go out, Polly."

Smiley's voice was monotone, but Polly was not deceived and knew he attempted to mask his fury.

She put her hand on the door handle, but before she could even open it, the captain had crossed the room and had her by the throat. He pushed her against the wall. "You betrayed me," he hissed in her face. "After all I've done for you!"

Polly tried to pull his hands away, but to no avail. She started gasping for breath as his fingers tightened.

"Why?" he screamed in her face. When it was obvious she couldn't reply he loosened his grip.

She choked, and tears streamed down her face. The first time she had cried in over thirty years. "My brother…" she finally spluttered.

"What?" His shock caused him to release her, and she fell against the wall panting, her hands to her throat.

Just then, Snake-Eye came charging in through the kitchen door. "Cap'n, he's been spotted by the men, Cutter has set the signal to say they're on his trail."

The tide was on its way in as Connie rushed across the sands with excitement brimming over. For on the way here she had half-decided to leave with Eddie. She was on the walkway up to the inn when she heard Smiley shouting. Instinct made her rush beyond the inn and up to the top of the island. She would wait until he was calm before going in search of Polly.

A scream pierced the air and filled her with dread. For a moment she stared at the inn, and then fled to the huer's hut. She would wait until it was quiet before venturing out. Another scream pierced the air, and now tears streamed down her cheeks, for in her soul she knew it was Polly that was being attacked. Smiley's voice roared and carried across the island, she caught something about Hawkins, but could make nothing else out. Everything went silent for a short while. Oh, that it had remained silent, but alas it did not. Polly, being chased by a crazed man, fled the inn and ran up the island. His hat was missing, his coat flew open. In both hands he held a pistol. Connie gasped, and then threw her hands over her mouth to cover the sound.

Polly raced beyond the hut and came to a grinding halt at the edge of the cliff. Connie sank on the floor and buried her face in her knees, covering her ears with her hands.

A muffled argument reached her, but she could understand none of it.

Polly had used the intrusion as her chance of escape. She bolted through the door, and would have headed for land, but Vera Brave and Spike were rushing towards the inn. She turned and fled up to the top of the island. She heard Smiley's cuss and his heavy footfall as he pursued.

Polly's flight had put upon him a rage that drowned sensibility and drove him with an uncontrollable blur of red rage to pursue the only woman he had ever loved, with a pistol in both hands. "Where do you think you're going woman? There's no escape up there."

She heard, and knew the truth of it, but despair compelled her to keep on. She ran until she reached the highest point. Standing on the edge, she realized her folly, there was no way down. A jump, which she had briefly considered, would lead only to rocks and death. She turned.

Smiley stood a short distance away. Behind him, no more than a shimmering light, hovered the ghost of Tom Crocker. Polly knew as soon as she saw the image of the dead pirate that her time was up.

"You've meant more to me than any other person."

"I know, and I have loved you like no other."

"Why? Why have you put me in this position Polly?" His voice was gravelly and gruff as he crushed the pain in his chest.

"He saved me once, he called repayment on me."

"You should have talked to me."

"I know."

Tom Crocker glided forward; almost becoming one with Smiley, for a split-second it seemed that two faces occupied the same space.

Bang!

The single shot hit her in the chest. For a moment, all he saw was her shocked face, and then she fell. Falling to a crushing death, no more would Polly Pretty-lips-hits-with-her-fists smile with those voluptuous lips, or her fists smash against another face. No more would she sail the seas and go plundering with her one true love.

Bang!

A scream – that curdled Connie's insides, and would never be forgotten.

Silence.

Connie shook, she tried hard to still her breath, but she found it hard to breathe. Tears coursed down her cheeks unchecked.

Her friend. Her friend.

She didn't know how long she stayed there, but the tide was in by the time it was dark enough for her to try and leave. All was quiet in the inn, and she knew any sound would alert the people within that she was there. There was a pain in her chest that made her think she was going to die, but she carried on, one slow step at a time.

She was barely able to wade through the sea to reach land, at one point the water came right up to her chest. Its cold mingled with her fright and shivers came upon her harshly, as she prayed the strong currents wouldn't wash her out to sea.

She had only one thought, and that was to reach Eddie before Smiley found her.

The coastal trail was hard going. She was drenched and her clothes weighed her down and dragged along the ground. Her teeth chattered and her hands shook, but from more than just the cold… Connie felt eyes on her back.

She constantly looked behind her expecting to find Smiley and his men descending on her. When the trail became shingle and stone she knew the approach of someone would be announced, but where it merged into a soft mix of sand and grass she knew she'd not give her presence away. Shivers ran down her spine and made her twist every now and again to look behind and to search the path back to the island. Nothing but the rustle of the breeze through tall grass reached her ears. And yet… the feeling persisted and uneasiness grew heavier and heavier.

An owl's hoot echoed over the land making her jump. She grabbed her middle as sickness washed through her.

By the time she arrived at the hut, Connie looked like a madwoman. She flew into Eddie's arms sobbing.

It took a long time for her to settle enough to be able to talk. Eddie tried to remain patient, but as time wore on his patience grew slim. He wasn't used to women, other than a quick tumble in a tavern room, so he found the tears hard to handle. After a while she sensed his rigidness, and pulled herself from his arms.

Eddie passed her a cup of cider, and when she had drunk it all he said, "Tell me."

A precious element, filled with sparkling secrets, Connie was strong and resourceful, anything but hysterical. So seeing her like this sent shivers down his spine. He had been in fear for his life numerous times, but nothing compared to the terror he now felt as he witnessed the woman he had come to love falling apart.

She began to tell him of Polly's brutal murder, with wide eyes and fluttering hands. "Polly... it's Polly."

"What is? What's happened?" When she didn't answer straight away, he shook her. "Tell me!"

"Murdered," she sobbed and threw herself once more upon his chest.

Eddie wrapped his arms around her as he tried to digest her news. When her sobs eased a little, he asked her, "Who done it, Connie?"

"Smiley! Smiley shot her on the island. I was in the huer's hut. As I looked out, I saw him pointing his pistol at her. Then she fell over the edge. Oh, Eddie, I dropped to the floor and covered my mouth to prevent my screams. I should have saved her, I should have gone out."

Eddie tightened his arms around her. "I'm mighty glad you didn't, otherwise you'd be dead beside her right now."

Connie knew the truth of it, but still she believed she had betrayed her only friend by not trying to help her, it caused her to sob the more. Heart-wrenching sobs flowed from her again, and for some time she was inconsolable. All the while, Eddie was planning.

Needing her to calm down, Eddie coaxed, "Hush now, hush."

At last, when her sobs were merely gasps for breath, he sat her down on a stool and knelt before her.

Clasping her hands with his, he looked at her, his eyes imploring her to be calm.

She settled eventually. "He must have found out she helped you, well us... no me. He found out and he killed her for her betrayal. It's all my fault! Her death is on my hands." Her voice had been rising in notches and quick to prevent another break down he wrapped his arms around her and held on tight.

"We must leave." He pushed her back a little to look into her eyes.

They gazed upon each other, with Eddie pleading silently. "It is not your fault; take that from your mind straight away. But Connie, if this is the truth... and I believe you, we must depart from here at once. No more can you tarry on your decision. Staying here is now impossible for you if you want to stay alive. If Smiley can kill his partner, he'll run you through without a second thought."

Connie let out a cry of fright.

Eddie searched her eyes. "You're a strong woman, Connie Boyton, you can do this. I know you want to grieve, and you'll have time aplenty for it once we are gone. But for now we must make haste. Do you understand?"

She nodded.

"Are there any ponies for sale hereabouts?"

His words exuded anxiety and she wished she could deliver better news. "I know of none," she replied. "Most farmers have packhorses to take produce to markets, or Shires for ploughing, but none will part with them."

He would have stolen one, but that would immediately show Connie he was incapable of change. "It'll take too long to walk to Liverpool, and we can't risk the highways."

"There's an inn at Ringmore; I've heard that many travelers rest there a while. If anyone would have a horse for sale it would be the innkeeper there."

"Then to Ringmore we must go."

"But we'll need money, of which we have none."

Eddie grinned. "Not exactly true." He put on his long coat, and opened the flaps to her. At first she didn't see anything, so he pointed. She followed his finger and realized it had secret pockets throughout the whole lining. "Pirates never know when they'll 'ave to flee, so we like to keep our goods upon our person. In each tuck I have a little something, enough to buy a horse, some new clothes for us, and maybe a night or two in an inn. I wish it was enough for passage to the New World too, but alas it will not stretch that far."

"To Ringmore then," she said.

"Is your husband at home?"

"He is."

"Then we cannot return for a change of clothes for you. There's a good chance you'll catch a chill."

"Then you'll need to tend to me, pirate of mine."

"And do it gladly I will!"

He reached out his hand. She looked at it and recognized she was at a major crossroads in her life. There would be no coming back, if Smiley didn't kill her then Joseph surely would. She slipped her freezing hand into his.

"But you are already so cold!"

"If we run I will become warm."

"You must take off your clothes and wear mine. We'll carry yours with us and when they're dry you can put them back on."

She wanted to be outraged at such a scandalous suggestion, but she realized the sense of it. "I don't need all your clothes, just your coat and belt."

He raised an eyebrow. "And all my worldly goods."

"Don't be lacking in brains now, Edmond Calstock, I could never outrun you and well you know it – limp or not."

He took off his coat and his belt.

Connie nodded her head towards the door. "Outside please."

He shook his head, but did as she requested and went outside for her to undress in privacy.

"When we're married you'll have to disrobe in front of me," he called over his shoulder.

"I'm not marrying you, Edmond Calstock, ever!"

"Don't you want to be an honest woman?"

"Are you less honest than me, because as far as I know – and I have heard your life history in *great detail*, you're not married?"

"There's no equality between us, and as a man I may do as I please and none will think the worse of me. You on the other hand…"

"Still don't want to marry you."

She came out then and Eddie whistled. "Look mighty fine you do."

She'd kept her knee-length fisherman's boots on because they wouldn't get far if she was in bare feet, though she'd removed her woolen stockings and tipped the excess water out of her boots. Her clothes she had tied into a bundle using her underskirt as a carrier. His coat nearly wrapped around her twice and fell way below her knees. Cinched in at the waist by his belt, it served well as a black leather dress.

"You look like Dick Whittington; we only need to attach your bundle to a stick, though of course you're a sight more tempting than he ever was."

"I think you should stop your flowery conversation. The tide will be on its way out again before dawn, and we need to be long gone by then."

"You're right. Here, give me that." Eddie took her bundle of clothes in one hand, and then took her hand in his other. "So I don't lose you in the dark," he said with a wink.

For the briefest of moments, a flicker of a smile touched her lips. And then the weirdest of things... she thought she saw Polly.

"Polly?" she cried out and tried letting go of Eddie's hand.

He held on and wouldn't let go. "It's only a trick of the moonlight, Connie, nothing more. Come on, let's go."

He pulled her away with him, but she kept craning her neck to look back across the warren, she was so sure she had seen her friend.

To stop her from looking back and pulling on his arm, Eddie asked a question to bring her back to their plight. "How long will it take us to reach this inn?"

It worked. She looked forward. "On a fair day the walk is but an hour, but in the dark I am worried about losing the path and it might take a little longer. They will not open their doors until daybreak at any rate, and we shall have reached it long before then."

They arrived outside the Cox's Inn before first light. With no lamplight gleaming through the windows they knew there was no point knocking on the door. They went a short distance and took shelter under a massive oak. Eddie pulled off Connie's boots and gave a low whistle when he saw her bloody feet.

"We've only been walking a little while, what will become of your feet after days of walking?"

"Firstly, isn't that why we're here, to buy a horse or pony? And secondly, my feet are hardy; it is only the saltwater that has hardened the leather and made it so tough it has scratched my poor feet to bits. Tomorrow, when my stockings are dry and the leather softened once more, it will not be so bad."

Eddie sat back against the tree and pulled Connie into his arms. She laid her head against his chest and within a minute fell into an exhausted sleep.

Chapter 12

IT HAD TAKEN EDDIE a while to fall asleep, his leg ached even though the wound was healing well, and Connie, unmoving, had become a weight that pinned him down preventing him from shifting his position. He could have turned her onto the ground he knew, but he wanted her to sleep in comfort and to allow time to begin the ebbing of the shock she carried.

Connie woke with the very first ray of light. Everything was instantly remembered causing a riot of emotions. It wasn't the loss of home comforts that made her catch her breath; it was the sudden expanse that separated her from everything that was familiar. She was a ship without an anchor, drifting into the great unknown. She didn't feel brave or adventurous. No, it was her stupidity that danced before her eyes. Love could never be secure, nor could Eddie be the rescuer of her battered soul. She needed to wake up from this dream of escape that lulled her into trusting a pirate.

She tried to disengage herself without waking him, but the moment she moved his eyes flew open. They looked at each other in the soft glow of morning, studying one another with their private thoughts.

"You look better this morning." It was true – her face was calm, and a rosy glow had crept upon her cheeks the moment he had looked at her, masking the purple bruises on her right cheek.

"Wet or not, I need to put my own clothes back on. For a pirate and a slattern would never be welcomed in a respectable establishment."

He chuckled. "What a shame that is, for I think you look rather fetching."

Connie took her bundle of soaking clothes and went behind the hedgerow to change. Putting on the freezing drenched clothes was not only horrible but difficult and a patter of irritation fell from her lips.

Eddie tried to keep the laughter from his voice, for her choice of words had greatly amused him. "Do you need a hand?"

"No!"

When she came around the hedge, she looked a sorrowful sight. Her clothes clung to her like limpets on a rock.

"We'd best find you some other clothes toot sweet mademoiselle!"

Connie scrunched up her face.

"It's something Pierre used to say." Still seeing her puzzled face, he elaborated. "He was a French pirate, it means quickly Miss."

"Toot sweet madam-seller, I like it!"

Eddie chortled, and didn't bother correcting her.

They'd only taken a few steps when Eddie said, "To cover our tracks we'll tell everyone you're heading for London and I'm escorting you."

"But we're not?"

"No, there are many more ships in Liverpool and we'll go unhindered there. It would be hard for anyone looking for us to find us there."

They went across the narrow lane to the arched oak door that was the entrance. Straight away, they knew someone was awake and busy. A billboard had been placed in the lane that announced: a bed for fourpence a night, no more than five can sleep in one bed, no boots to be worn in bed, no razor grinders or tinkers taken in, no dogs allowed in the kitchen, and organ grinders to sleep in the wash house!

"There's no mention where pirates can sleep," Connie pointed out with a grin.

"Nor whether they permit entrance to drowned rats!" Eddie ducked, for the entrance was low, pushed the door open, and went inside.

Connie, though she was three and twenty, had only ever set foot in the Pilchard Inn and the Sloop, and only then on Joseph's orders. Following Eddie into the lounge, she was struck by the comfort of it. Not only was it enormous compared to the Pilchard and the Sloop, but it oozed a certain richness to which she was unaccustomed. Dark red wood, on floors, walls and counters, had been polished to a shine. Over the enormous opening of the stone fireplace an assortment of brass pots hung, and she wondered if customers were expected to cook their own food. She expressed the thought to Eddie, who burst out laughing.

"No, they're simply for ornamentation; there'll be a cook in the kitchen to create adequate meals for patrons."

There was a rich powerful smell of old ale and tobacco, but not so that it made her want to hold her nose as it did in the other two inns. As her eyes drank in the deep red cushions on the chairs and the bottles standing behind the bar, the innkeeper came rushing forward.

"Well met good sir." Though his words were ordinary and customary, the tone held a note of rejection that made Connie cringe. He was short and stout and yet somehow managed to look down his stumped nose at the two of them, who stood head-and-shoulders above him. After looking them up and down, and not hiding his displeasure at their company, (compelled by habit and custom) he inquired, "How might I serve you today?"

Connie wanted to leave, but Eddie was unfazed.

"Good sir, we need many things as it happens, all of which I pray you'll be able to supply... and fear not I have coin enough for all our requests."

Perhaps the politeness of Eddie's voice had not been what he expected, or maybe Connie's sorrowful drenched and forlorn appearance had awoken his better judgment, whatever the reason, he suddenly smiled. "Sir, give me your list and I will do my very best."

Connie strolled to the fireplace, where she stretched out her hands greedy for its warmth, while the two men began a conversation that entailed a lot of bartering. Soon a price on all things requested, (except a horse) had been met, and hands had been shaken.

"Come this way, madam, I will show you to a room where you can wait while my good wife delivers to you some dry clothing."

Connie offered him a smile and gladly followed. Eddie perched himself on the edge of a stool and gave her a wink as she walked away. Her sigh caught the innkeeper's attention.

"I take it the *gentleman* is the cause of your distress," he remarked as he led her through a very narrow throughway.

"I'm not a woman of ill repute," she snapped.

"And I thought no such thing, beg my pardon if I gave you that impression."

He sounded genuine and Connie relented. "He's but a kind soul who has agreed to assist me with safe passage to London. There is nothing more betwixt us than that."

Eddie had told him something to the contrary, but he did no more than rise one eyebrow which she did not see.

"Indeed, it would be foolish for a woman on her own to travel the countryside, especially on foot. Here we are." He'd stopped outside a door and nodded towards it. "My Annie will be along shortly, and hopefully she will find something to fit you. Also, the gentleman requested you a washbasin and one will be brought along presently."

"Thank you, that would be appreciated."

Annie arrived a short while later with her arms full of clothes, informing Connie she carried a mixture of hers and her three daughters' clothes, and between them they'd surely find her something wearable. Having already washed and tied her hair in a bun at the back of her head by the time Annie arrived, she immediately set to work to find something to wear. A white blouse with ruffles was fine, although too big, Connie was able to tie a corset over the top and it fitted well enough. The skirts were all too large around the waist and she had to put Eddie's belt back on to hold a pale-blue one in place. Her boots had been placed by the fire to dry, and Annie whisked away her salt-soaked clothes for washing.

She made her way back to the lounge in bare feet and looked around for Eddie. A couple of gentlemen sat at different tables but she couldn't see him anywhere. "Excuse me," she called to a serving girl. "Have you seen Eddie... I mean, a tall man with long very curly hair." She couldn't bring herself to say 'and dressed like a pirate,' so she stopped there.

The girl shook her head and went on her way.

Connie was swaying slightly, unsure of which direction to go. She played with the dry straw floor-covering with her toe and wondered where on earth Eddie had gone. Just then, a man approached her. Uncomfortable talking to strange men, she made a turn to go back to her room.

"Connie."

She stopped dead, she knew that voice. She turned around. Her jaw dropped. Eddie raised one eyebrow at her. "Acceptable, mam?"

His long locks had been trimmed and neatly tied in pigtail hanging from the nape of his neck, with only stray wisps appearing from under his hat. Gone were the mustache and chin beard, the colorful necktie, the frilly shirt and black waistcoat, and even his thigh-high boots. In fact, the only item of his original clothing left was his jacket which he carried over his arm.

Clean-shaven; wearing dark green knee-length breeches, white stockings, black shoes, and a well-tailored fitted jacket he was completely transformed. The only resemblance to the man she had known was the color of his hair and eyes, and that his skin was sun-kissed brown.

"Squire Tallow at your service, mam." He took off a very smart tri-corn hat and gave an elaborate bow.

"Tallow?"

"Yes, Miss Susannah Tallow. Your cousin, escorting you to London."

Connie giggled, she couldn't help herself. He offered her his arm and escorted her to a table in the corner of the room. He took the chair with his back to the wall, and Connie realized straight away he had positioned himself to be able to see everyone who entered the establishment. The thought that he was watching for Smiley tempered her short-lived merriment and she sat down more soberly.

Leaning across the table, in a hushed voice she said, "I don't think I like the name Susannah."

Eddie smiled. "It's only for a short time."

"When do we leave?"

"Your clothes are in the garden, airing on the line. Are you overly fond of them? If not, I suggest we break our fast and then be on our way leaving your clothes behind."

"You have a horse then?"

He shook his head, and pulled his mouth to one side. "Unfortunately not. Apparently there are none for sale, and we must make our way to Modbury if we want one. Alternatively, he has told me of a post carriage that might carry us from

Ivybridge to London for a very small fare and... as he's not supposed to pick up passengers, our trip with him will remain secret. We would alight a long way before we reach the city and then make our way to Liverpool. I vote we do that, what say you?"

"I get a vote?"

Eddie's face grew solemn. "Yes of course, whatever you want Connie, that is what we'll do."

"You mean... Cousin Susannah?" But she was smiling. For a moment she forgot that Polly had recently gone to meet her maker, or that as a fisherman's wife she had no right to be making her own plans or traveling with a stranger.

"Where shall we go Cousin Susannah, and how shall we travel?"

In this precise moment she didn't care. Lost in Eddie's eyes all she could think about was how much she wanted him to kiss her again.

Her longing for him was clearly on display, her chest rose and fell in a quick manner and her eyes had glazed over.

He wanted to reach over and take her hand, but a quick look around reminded him they were not alone, and hand-holding was not something cousins should do.

"I have a map," he said spreading a small parchment upon the table. "The innkeeper tells me if we follow this way..." he ran his finger along a line. Both of them leaned forward across the table to peer down at the map, their heads nearly touching. Eddie inched closer to her ear and whispered, "I'll look after you Connie, I swear. I'll do everything in my power to make you happy. Be my wife; let me show you what a marriage should be like."

Connie sat back in her chair. He saw by the set of her chin that she would decline. "You don't trust me, I know. In truth, we hardly know each other, so 'tis 'ard for me to explain that I just know that we should be together. I believe if you give me a chance I could make you happy."

"I'm already a wife, as well you know. I might not attend church any more, but I still know what is right. And having two husbands is not."

"Then I must be content to have you as my mistress, umm, in fact, I rather like the sound of that!"

She kicked him hard under the table, though being barefooted she hurt her toes more than his shins. Her eyes smarted with pain, but she kept blinking, not allowing any tears to show.

"So, not a wife nor a mistress, this will make for an interesting journey will it not?"

"Surely not, cousin, it appears to me most mundane."

"Arr, here comes food, thank heavens for that."

The innkeeper placed two plates on the table, each overflowing with eggs and bacon, and buttered bread.

"Thank you," they both said.

A short while later they paid the innkeeper for his neighbor's smart green outfit, his wife's clothes, the food and use of the room, and after putting back on her almost dry boots, then they were on their way.

Thankfully, it was a sunny morning and although clouds floated above, they didn't appear to be rain filled.

They had walked a distance in silence, listening to birdsong and an occasional moo from the herds they passed. Primroses lined the road and reminded them that spring was leaving and summer drifted closer.

Eddie started whistling, a tune she did not know. It sounded merry and she was curious. "What tune is that?"

"It's a sailor's song, it tells of how a sailor has a wife in every port."

Connie couldn't help laughing.

"Egad, but you're beautiful when you smile."

They stopped walking and regarded one another.

It felt to Connie as if Eddie sucked her soul into his with his beautiful blue eyes and cheeky smile. Alas, his disarming smile, more deadly than a cutlass, would not make her a victim to his charms; of this, she was quite determined! Yet his ocean-deep eyes beckoned her to lean forward, to enter his space, and submit to the lust that suddenly flooded his eyes and filled his whites with tiny red veins.

She pulled back. "You're not the first man to make those pretty eyes at me, and if you think you're irresistible, well I tell you, you're nothing but foolish and delusional!"

He thumped his fists against his chest with a dramatic turn-downed mouth, and head cocked to the left. "Oh, fair lady you wound me mortally… these 'pretty eyes' have lured women, too many for me to count, into my arms – you mean *all* of them were blind?"

"You're a scoundrel!"

For a moment they looked at each other, and then a blast of laughter poured between them.

When her laughter subsided, she squinted and scrutinized him critically. With more beauty than any man should possess, and with a silver-tongue he presented her with the biggest challenge of her life, for to resist him was becoming unbearably hard.

For the first time in seven years, she was open and not having to measure her words. Was it that she had saved his life, and now partly believed he belonged to her? She considered this a real possibility.

The sound of racing horses made them pull apart from each other and look forward. Charging towards them were three masked men.

"Stand and deliver!" the first rider called as he pulled his horse to a stop in front of them.

"You've got to be jesting?" snapped Eddie.

"You're either blind or without brains for we have neither carriage nor horse and we're already standing, and obviously have no wealth!" snapped Connie.

"There is no time for merriment or sarcasm, my friends," said the first rider slipping from his saddle to approach them. He held a pistol and aimed it at them. "I am sure you do not wish me to take the life of this lovely young woman. So... promptly hand over your goods."

The second rider also alighted and pointed a pistol at them.

Connie stepped closer to him, and Eddie was aware that her life was in his hands and with no guns he could hardly protect her. He reached inside his coat.

"Steady!" warned the highwayman.

"I'm reaching for my purse." The masked man nodded towards him, and Eddie slowly pulled out his money pouch.

The second highwayman took it from him, and bounced the bag in his hand. "There's not much here," he said.

"I'm sure if you didn't want slim pickings that you'd keep to the highways, for only humble folk would walk these lanes," replied Eddie.

The second highwayman looked at the first, who jerked his head indicating the man should return to his horse. With all three mounted once more, the first rider tipped his hat. "Good day to you and a pleasant and safe journey I wish you." The three laughed and then went galloping off down the lane.

"Blaggards!" cussed Connie.

"Probably cousins of the innkeeper at the Cox's," said Eddie.

She looked at him shocked. "Do you think so? In which case, we should return at once!"

"We couldn't prove it, even if they were sitting within, for their faces were covered. He probably thought that as a pirate I would have riches hidden on me." Eddie sat down on the wayside.

Connie joined him, "What do we do now? If that was the bulk of your funds, we will find it hard to reach Liverpool without a long and hungry walk."

"I exchanged my medallion for that purse of coins. I must be cursed, you would be better off to leave me and make your own escape. Here, I'll give you the only thing of value I have left. Use it and go in search of a safe place to live. You're better off alone." He went inside his coat and brought out a signet ring. It was heavy and engraved with roses.

She refused to take it. "Do you always give up so easily, Edmond Calstock? Well, I thought more of you and that's for sure!"

"You can't beat fate. Maybe I was supposed to die that day like the rest of my crew. I've been on borrowed time and now I must surrender."

Full of irritation, Connie stood up. "Oh, stuff and nonsense, what dribble you talk! This is a setback, that's all. Come, let's get going, there's nothing to be gained by moaning on the roadside!"

"Go on without me I tell you." Eddie dropped his head onto his drawn-up knees.

Connie crouched beside him and placed a hand on his shoulder. "Don't despair Eddie, all will be well."

He looked up at her, and the sorrow in his eyes melted her heart. "I think this is my fault. When I knew the ship was done for, I had only one thought in my mind, and that to steal the bullion that belonged to us all. I didn't try and save my sea mates as they spilled over the side, no, I wanted only the gold that would settle my future. I lost it. I saved no one but myself and I even lost the gold, so what principle is there in that? Only that I'm a wretched man indeed."

Connie should have waited a moment and pondered her next sentence, instead without thought she blurted out, "And what if I knew where your gold is? Would you be happy then?"

He threw her a piercing stare and she straightened up and moved a step away from him. Eddie got slowly to his feet.

"Do you know where the chest is, Connie?"

Confusion filled her. She took another step back.

Eddie lurched forward, grabbed her shoulders and shook her hard. "Tell me, do you know where it lies?"

She nodded.

He gasped and let her go.

"Where?"

She took another step back.

"By God, Connie you'd better tell me where it is right now, or I'll..."

"Or you'll what? Give me a beating? Do your worst!"

Some of his anger released and tension drained out of him. "Never Connie, never would I hit you."

"Even if I stole your gold?"

"Even then."

They stood for a long moment assessing each other.

"I hid it at the back of the cave on the beach where I found you."

Eddie bit his lip and shook his head. "I can't believe it."

"It's there, I swear. I checked the day before yesterday and it was still there."

"No, I meant I can't believe you stole it from me."

"I'm sure if you find something then it becomes yours. Not my fault if you lost it."

"Firstly, finding something does not make it yours, and secondly did I lose it, or did you remove it from me?"

She colored.

Eddie shook his head. "I can't believe you didn't tell me, not even when we decided to run. With that chest we could start a new life in the Americas, we could buy land, Connie! Isn't that your dream? Why would you leave it behind?"

Connie's eyes were downcast; she couldn't face him and reveal the truth, so she concentrated on a rut in the road. "It was on the sand beside you, hanging by a loose cord. At first, I hid it with the plan of running away from Joseph and using the gold to buy a farm."

"And later?"

Connie wrapped her arms around her middle, but still wouldn't raise her face towards him. "Later that night, when I saw all the dead bodies I was sickened. They were slaughtered so that the pirates and the villagers could steal their goods. When I thought of the chest after that it only made me feel sick."

"We have to go back."

"No!" Connie's head sprung up, with dismay written all over it. "They'll kill us, Joseph and Smiley, one of them, they'll slit our throats."

"I'm sure Joseph wouldn't murder his own wife, and as for Smiley and his crew we'll just have to ensure they don't find us."

Connie shook her head with a flurry of sharp turns. "No, no, I can't do it, I won't do it."

"Then stay here, find somewhere to hide. When I 'ave the chest I'll come back for you."

She rushed at him and grabbed his arm. "No, Eddie please, please don't go back."

His face softened, he reached over and tucked a piece of stray hair behind her ear. "I'll come back for you, I swear it. Meet me back in this very spot tomorrow at the same time as now, and we'll embark on an adventure together." He dropped his hand then, stepped around her, and strode back along the way they had come.

She stared at his back in horror. The pirates would kill him. This would be the last time she saw him. Tears of apprehension and stress raced down her cheeks. He grew smaller as the distance between them increased.

"I don't want you to be dead, Edmond Calstock."

As she finished saying his name, prickles hit her back and she knew someone or something was watching. Thud-thud went her heart as she turned with agonizing slowness. No one was there, but goosebumps made the hairs on her arm prickle. She spun around, hitched up her skirts, and started racing up the lane after her pirate.

Chapter 13

THEY BYPASSED BIGBURY and stayed off the lanes as much as possible. They'd drunk water from a stream, but they wouldn't risk being seen by anyone for a chance of food. They made good time in spite of Eddie's slight limp, the prospect of getting his hands back on the gold, urged him forward with great speed. The clouds had darkened overhead, and the wind had picked up. Another storm was coming. They hoped they could reach the beach and be gone before it hit.

Each step closer to Bigbury-on-Sea they took filled Connie with dread. She had always told herself that Joseph didn't frighten her, but she knew that was a lie. The possibility he would kill her, even if by too much violence and not by intent, was very real and she compared her misgivings and apprehension to that of an accused man walking towards the gallows.

They were hiding in a coppice on the edge of the warren near Connie's beach.

"If you tell me where your secret path over the cliff lies, I can be there and back in no time. You stay 'ere, and remain hidden."

"You can't go now, it's too exposed; somebody may see you."

"There ain't anyone 'ere.

"But if the fishermen are out, they'll see you for sure. We need to wait until it's dark."

"We'll be walking in the night again. It'll be 'ard going."

"Yes, but at least we'll be going! If you go now we might get caught."

"Then let's find some shelter to rest a while. Should we go back to the shepherd's hut?"

"No, Joseph will be watching for me, he knows I go there sometimes, he may have set someone to keep a lookout."

"Then let's go deeper into the woods and find a place of high ferns."

Deep inside the cover of trees, they came to a small clearing. When Eddie observed the whiteness of Connie's face, compassion flooded him. "I'll protect you. He'll not hurt you I promise."

"That's a promise you shouldn't make for you don't know what lies ahead of us."

"You told me you know how to shoot, but do you know how to protect yourself without a weapon?"

She shook her head.

"Then let me show you a few simple moves, so if you're attacked you might put up a good fight."

Connie loved the idea of defending herself. "Teach me!"

They spent a little time mock fighting. Eddie instructed Connie on different ways to steady her balance and how to use her fists to fight back. With everything that had been happening though, Connie soon tired and asked to stop.

Surprising herself, Connie went to sleep as soon as they lay down among the moss and ferns. Eddie pulled her close and held her head against his chest. "You should 'ave told me about the gold," he whispered. He rubbed his nose in her hair and then kissed her forehead.

It was dark when Eddie shook Connie awake. She yawned and stretched, and then fixed him with a stare. "Did you manage to sleep?"

"A little."

He took her hand and the two of them stepped with caution until they'd reached the wood's edge. They stood for a long time watching and listening.

"I think we're safe to go," she said at last.

"Not us, you stay 'ere. Just point me in the right direction."

"It'll take you too long to find the steps down to the beach. I'll take you, come on."

They ran across the grasslands, both their heads swinging constantly from side to side as they searched for danger. By the time they reached the cliff edge, it had begun to drizzle.

"Does it always rain 'ere?" Eddie moaned.

"Often, but when the sun shines it is most beautiful. Damn!"

"What is it?"

"The tide's almost fully in, we'll have to go into the sea to reach the cave, and the currents are dangerous. We should wait until morning."

"We can't do that. Come on show me your path, I'll brave the sea."

Connie searched the edge until she found her path, and pointed.

"This is your way down?" he asked.

"Yes."

"I'll go, you stay 'ere and keep a lookout. If you see anyone coming, slip over the edge yourself and we'll hide until they've gone. Can you whistle?"

She shook her head. "Never mind, just come over the edge and when I come out of the cave I'll see you. And you're sure no one but you knows the chest is here?"

"No one."

"You didn't tell Polly?"

She shook her head again.

He half turned to step over the edge, then stopped, and came back. He grabbed her face in his hands and planted a kiss on her lips. Her fingers went to touch her lips as soon as he turned towards the cliff again. He climbed over the edge and was gone. She tried listening for his steps but they seemed to have stopped. Suddenly, his head reappeared over the edge. He grinned at her when he saw her touching her mouth and she instantly dropped her hand away.

His arm swung up and he dropped his clothes on the grass. "I know it's beginning to rain," he said, "but they won't get so wet here as in the sea with me." He gave her a cheeky grin and disappeared once more. She heard him hiss when he went into the freezing water. After that, she heard no more. She hovered over the edge watching for him, but couldn't see or hear anything. Not wanting to stand immediately on top of her secret steps she moved along the coast a little; just enough to keep watching the path, but far enough away so as not to bring attention to it. She was so intent on watching for Eddie's return, that the wind masked the approach of heavy footfall.

Too late, she heard the crunch of feet behind her and spun just in time to see Joseph reaching for her.

*****

Inside the cave, Eddie was having a hard time finding the small shelf Connie had told him about. The waves were knocking him about and he kept losing his stance and falling into the sea. Again and again he rose, feeling along the cave's walls for the chest's hiding place. One wave sucked him under and he hit his elbow against a rock. He cussed, righted himself and continued with his search.

*****

"I knew you wouldn't have left Bigbury," fumed Joseph, shaking her like a ragdoll. "Where have you been? Why didn't you come home?" He shook her, making her head snap up and down. A dark cloud moved away from the moon and allowed its light to stream down on them. Joseph saw the defiance in her eyes, raised his hand and struck her across the face. "Where have you been?"

The devil took hold of Connie and she screamed back him, "As far away from you as I could get, you small-minded oaf!"

He lunged at her. Before she could react, his hands were around her neck squeezing the breath out of her. His foul alcohol-staled breath tinged her nose, bringing with it the memories of his every beating and every promise of her demise.

*****

Eddie's hand found something... a ledge! He realized straight away it was dry. It was pitch-black in the cave and he wished for the hundredth time that he could have had a lamp with him. His feet found a ledge below the water and he stood on it. Now he was only waist deep in the sea. There! His hand hit a box.

"Now, my friend, we just have to get out of here in one piece."

*****

With murderous intent, Joseph gripped her slim throat in his large, calloused hands. He squeezed and his face took on the image of Lucifer. Sparks flew before Connie's eyes, as she tried to pull his hands away from her neck.

His face contorted with the expression of a crazed man. His eyes were fully bloodshot, and sweat rolled from his forehead and mingled with raindrops. He glared into her eyes as he increased the pressure and shook her in the process.

Her life had been a nightmare of pain and eternal torture, yet she grasped at it with all her might. She wanted to live! For the first time since Joseph Boyton had made her his wife – Connie fought back.

Maybe it was the unexpectedness of her kicks and thumps, or maybe it was the volume of alcohol in his blood, whatever the cause, Joseph let go of her neck and stumbled backwards in surprise. He seemed dazed, suddenly confused. Then his eyes darkened once more and focused on her face. "You are a dead woman!" He lunged towards her, his long arms before him. His giant hands reached for her neck… that already colored purple.

Connie put her right foot back and bent her knees the way Eddie had shown her a few hours ago. "No!" she screamed, raising both hands at the same time to push and block him. His attack halted, but only for a second, then he ground his teeth, snarled and came again.

"No!" She pushed him again, this time with all her might. Joseph was used to throwing punches, not defending himself, and her thrusts knocked him off balance. He staggered two steps backwards, the cliff now but one more step away. Before he could get his full balance, she charged at him, all the years of built-up hatred poured power into her fists. With both hands clenched into fists she punched him in the chest.

His arms pin-wheeled in the air as he swayed and fought for his balance, then he took another step backwards.

Connie's arms dropped to her side. She knew without a shadow of a doubt what was coming. She should have reached for him, steadied him, pulled him back from the edge, but she didn't. She watched. Coldness along with satisfaction crept upon her face... she smirked with the waggishness of a crazed woman. In that precise moment, the heavy build of her husband disappeared over the edge. There was no need to see if he lived. No one could survive that steep fall onto the rocks below. "I forgive you!" she cried over the cliff.

Sorrow should have clawed at her spirit, remorse even more so. Sadness? However, none of those things filled her. Instead, she was full of joy. She was free at last, truly and absolutely free.

"No one will ever dominate me like that again!" she declared to the waves crashing against the rocks below.

Then to her utter dismay, a shimmer of light flickered in front of her view. For one mad moment, she thought her husband had grown wings, and was coming back to finish what he had started. She blinked, willing the light to be a figment of her imagination and be gone. But alas, when she opened them again, there before her hung the drenched shimmering image of Polly. Floating just out of reach, but at face level, so that Connie could stare into her blank white face and know that she had finally gone mad.

Connie tottered a step forward, her body swaying as if she was a ship on high waves. "Polly," she cried, "have you come to fetch me to the next world?" Her friend did not reply; she looked like she would speak but could not move her lips. Her arms reached out as if to embrace Connie.

Connie knew now she was on the brink of madness. She had murdered her husband, and already her penance called to her. As Polly's translucent hands reached for her, she screamed. The sound ripped from her throat – more shrill a sound there never had been. Terror, fear and loss, all merged into a ball of pain that demanded release.

*****

On Burr Island, Smiley and his crew heard the scream.

"Fetch the rowing boat, Spike, I think we need to see what's afoot."

*****

A sudden strong gust came from nowhere and Connie's cloak flew unexpectedly behind her and caused her to lose her uncertain balance. She wavered on the edge as she fixed her gaze on the face of her dead friend. She thought she heard Polly call out her name, but still her lips remained firmly closed as she stared at her with huge white eyes that had lost all color from both pupil and iris.

"Forgive me!" Connie cried and her foot moved closer to the edge. Still, the apparition did not leave and madness nudged the edge of Connie's mind and drove her to take yet another step towards her doom. Now her toes perched precariously on the tip of the granite cliff; to follow her husband – what a fitting end!

"Connie!"

She heard her name called as if from a great distance and fancied Polly was calling her from the other side of life, beyond the grave, and the thought made her laugh in an insane manner. She spread her arms wide, the breeze causing her cloak and hair to flow behind her. "Let madness take me," she cried to the heavens. "I care not to live with such sorrow and guilt."

In the precise moment when she leaned forward into the blustery sea breeze and prepared to fly to her death – destiny intervened.

Eddie managed to grab her wrist just as she toppled over the edge.

She fell.

Caught by Eddie's firm hand, her body crashed into the cliff face, and there she hung like a fly from a spider's thread.

Her arm rebelled against the sudden jar, and pain shot from it and crashed into her senses. Her cry of agony revived her from sorrow's madness, and now she saw clearly that she still wanted to live!

With panic-filled eyes, she glanced up at the man who held her life in his hands.

"I've got you," Eddie said. By then Eddie was lying on the ground. He reached towards her with his other hand. She grasped it with her free hand; panic now a tight band around her chest that was trying to steal her breath.

Eddie's face was marble, masking the fact that he was terror-stricken. He started edging backwards, inching her upwards. Her feet scrambled around the rock face searching for footholds.

Finally, her toes found one. She pushed, he pulled, and with one last heave she was once more back on solid ground.

She scrambled into his arms, every part of her shaking. "Has she gone?"

"Who?"

"Polly, has she gone?"

Eddie's heart skipped a beat before pounding fiercely against his ribs. Connie had looked crazed before she fell. What if she had lost her mind, what could he do except take her to an asylum?

"There's no one 'ere my girl," he hushed, as he held her head close to his chest. Connie wept, and Eddie let her, but as soon as she slowed her sobs, he pushed her from him and looked into her eyes.

She didn't seem crazy.

"I need to get dressed, and we 'ave to go, it's too dangerous 'ere."

She blinked and gave a nod, and the two of them got shakily to their feet. At any other time her obvious lack of interest in his nakedness would have amused him, now it only confirmed that her mind was slipping away.

"What were you doing so close to the edge?" Eddie asked tenderly, as he pulled on his breeches in haste.

The murder and the ghostly visit poured from her like soured milk. Eddie could hardly believe what he was hearing, and wondered what frightened him the most, the fact that his love could murder someone or that she was haunted by the loss of her friend.

*****

Though the pirates searched throughout most of the night, they couldn't find the cause of the scream. It was the early hours of the following day that they discovered Joseph's broken body on the rocks.

"Well it wasn't him that did scream as if he was being pulled into Hades," muttered Spike.

"No indeed, I agree, it could be no other than Connie that screamed like that. It appears she has had enough of his beatings."

"This is village business then," said Bill Bones. "I'll go and let them know." Bill waited for Smiley to confirm.

"Yes, you tell them…"

"Cap'n?" said Bill, for he could see that something troubled Smiley and his mind was running a hundred thoughts.

"They'd been hitched together for many a year, I can't help but wonder on the cause of her uncharacteristic boldness. What is it that gave her such courage all of a sudden?"

"What ya thinking, Cap'n?" asked Snake-Eye.

"I'm thinking that we have two missing pirates, and that either one of them could be helping her. Why would they help a fisherman's wife I ask myself? And the only answer I can come up with is that she found the doubloons or the treasure map or even both."

Chapter 14

EDDIE HAD HALF-DRAGGED Connie away from the cliff and along the coastal trail, he didn't know how long they had been running, but he did know he had no idea where they were going. Thankfully, the shower that threatened, had passed with the force of wind, and left them only damp and not soaked.

"Connie!" He cupped her face in his hands. "Connie you need to revive yourself and tell me which way we should go."

He could see she resisted, longing to stay in the state of stupor she was in, hiding from grief and shock. "Come on my girl, you can do this."

Bit-by-bit she focused. "Where do we head?" she asked, though her voice seemed faint and her mind still far away.

"Let's try for Modbury. If along the way we come across a horse for sale, that'll serve us well. At least we know we 'ave a good chance to find one there. Then we'll make haste for Liverpool. Having studied the map the innkeeper gave me, I think it'll take us the best part of three or four days to reach Liverpool, as long as we can buy a horse that is."

Connie looked around and tried to recognize where they stood, for in truth she had not been paying attention to anything since the cliff's edge. At last, a familiar stone row reminded her of a footpath that ran between the farms. As it was too small for carriages or carts, only people on foot or horseback could navigate them. "That way," she said pointing.

Eddie held onto her hand tightly and they set off again. The chest under Eddie's other arm shook from time to time and the coins did jingle. Connie started fixating on their noise and a hatred for the coins rose in her.

"You should throw them away!"

"This gold will buy our future, Connie."

"That gold is tainted by blood and will bring us nothing but bad fortune. Do you think Smiley will stop looking for it?"

"As far as he knows, it's lying at the bottom of the sea."

They had walked a short distance more, when Connie squeezed Eddie's hand.

"What is it?" he asked.

"We're being followed."

"I've been constantly checking, I swear no one follows."

"I can feel them." Connie's voice was a high-pitched squeal.

Eddie felt frantic, not of pursuers but of Connie losing her mind. "You're thinking *his* ghost is coming for you, aren't you?" He bit on his thumb while he waited her answer.

"Oh no!" she cried, "no, 'tis not that." She shook her head, her damp, loose curls bouncing off her shoulders. "This feeling started a long time back. In fact, within hours of Polly's…"

Eddie searched her face as he tried to work out what it was she thought followed them. "But you've not actually seen anyone following you, or us?"

"No, I've been quick to turn many a time, but I've never seen anyone."

"Probably only the wind then, it do whistle across the coast in an eerie fashion."

"Could be." She wasn't convinced, but she said nothing more. What she didn't confess to him, was that always in her peripheral view the wispy apparition of her friend floated with tenacious foreboding. If she told Eddie she was being haunted by Polly Fists he might abandon her, and who could blame him? The craziness of it kept a giggle bubbling in her chest, which she squashed with all her power. She had seen the concern in Eddie's eyes and now a panic that he would leave her mingled with her terror of the spectre that followed in her wake.

Misunderstanding the look on her face, Eddie said, "There's no going back. Joseph's body will deliver you to the hangman as sure as I'm stood here. Not a person in the village will think you innocent; your beatings at his hands must be common knowledge, for it was plain to my eyes and must be to theirs."

"I know."

"Then why are you so melancholy? Are you not free at last?"

"I've left myself behind in Bigbury-on-Sea. I'll never again see through the eyes of my innocence. I'm a different woman."

"Are you regretful for saving my life, for that is when it all started did it not?"

"No, Eddie Calstock, I don't regret that. But if I have any wishes left, then it would be that we'd met seven years past and that you'd whisked me away before Joseph ever knocked on my door."

Eddie wrapped his arm around her shoulder. "Aye, me too, Connie Boyton, me too."

On wound the footpath through a darkened night and a silent land. Connie fancied she was not made for the adventurer's life after all, home even with all its problems and pain, seemed more familiar to her soul. Bigbury-on-Sea and Burr Island particularly, made for a coarse blanket that scratched her skin... yet offered her the comfort and warmth of familiarity. Escape from her lot in life had presented itself in none of the ways she had envisioned.

A single tear trickled down her cheek, 'let go and live' it implored, but she wiped it away in frustration. How could she ever be happy now that she was a murderer?

Thankfully, Polly had faded and Connie hadn't seen her for some time, with the pale light of dawn creeping over the land, she hoped she would never see her friend again. "God rest her soul," she muttered and made the sign of the cross over her chest.

"What did you say?" asked Eddie.

"I think I have to rest a while, can we do that?"

Eddie stopped walking immediately and turned to her. "Of course we can. Do you know where we are? Do you know anyone who might offer us respite for a while? They won't have heard about Joseph yet, so we should be alright."

"I have no friends beyond Bigbury-on-Sea, and maybe some in Bigbury itself. Honestly, this is further than I have ever wandered. Both as a child and as a wife I would have to be home before dark, so there was only so far I could roam."

"Your life has been small."

She wanted to retort back a biting remark about his life, but there was no fight left in her. If she wasn't thinking about letting Polly down, then she was remembering Joseph's face as he went over the cliff. She shuddered.

"You're cold, come let us find somewhere to rest and I'll warm you." He took her hand and led her further down the path. Where they were, the hedgerow was too thick to pass through. Shortly, they came to a stile. "Do you know where this leads?" he asked.

She shook her head.

"Let's find out." They climbed over the little wooden steps and entered a field of wildflowers. "Either this land is unclaimed, or it's being left to pasture for animals. Let's go to that line of trees over yonder."

Connie's steps became smaller, and the effort required to pick up her feet increased. Eddie smiled at her. "Not far now."

They arrived at the trees and made their way through them looking for a place of comfort and dryness. A babbling brook ran through and they drank by cupping their hands. Eddie led them to an ancient sycamore, so vast was its trunk that it would take four people touching hands to reach around it. Covered in rich green leaves with branches that hung low. Some of the tree's roots rose above the ground and sat exposed, if offered them a comfortable place to sit.

Eddie tucked the chest under his knees and invited Connie to sit next to him. She shook her head and sat within an arm's reach of him.

"Connie…"

"I don't want to talk about it."

As the sun crept into the sky, slight warmth worked its way into their cold bodies. Eddie meant to stay awake, but he was asleep almost instantly.

Connie longed for sleep, but it seemed that now her body could rest, her mind had become as sharp as a pin. As she listened to Eddie's heavy breathing, she pondered on what might lie ahead of them. She wanted none of the money, of that she was sure. What she couldn't decide was whether she would stay with Eddie or not. She looked at his face and wanted to touch his lips. The memory of his brief kisses still lingered on her lips. If things had been different, she would have done anything to be with him. But she had committed a crime, nay more than one… crimes. Although only one murder was on her hands, she had witnessed the murders of others and had done nothing to save them. She was a terrible person and deserving of punishment. She should seek the magistrates and turn herself in. Yes! That is what she would do.

As she crept away from the sleeping pirate, she held her breath expecting him to wake at any moment. She was surprised when he didn't stir. Once clear of the coppice she started running along a lane. It would no doubt lead her to a farmhouse soon and she would beg them to take her to the nearest town.

With it being daylight, she had given no thought to Polly, after all no one ever saw Tom Crocker except at night. When a shimmer of light reflected off the stones on the lane before her, she didn't give it too much thought but her pace slowed. When the shimmer began to take form and substance she stumbled on the path and crashed face down. In a flash, as a ball bounces, she was back on her feet, poised for flight. Floating in her way was the ghost of her friend.

"How can this be?"

Polly reached out a hand. Connie stumbled backwards, putting out a hand herself to ward the ghost away. Polly floated down the narrow lane. Heartbeat-thuds threatened to crack Connie's ribs. She took a step backwards.

"I'm sorry Polly, I'm sorry. I didn't mean to bring trouble to your door, and I should have helped you on the island, I'm sorry. Please forgive me."

The full image of Polly floated above the ground, fully dressed as the day she died. She looked real, yet her face looked nightmarish and terrifying. No color touched her face or the hands that reached for Connie.

Connie whimpered, "You're not real, you're not real." The apparition came closer. Connie fought for breath, gulping and trying to force air into her lungs, which seemed to have closed in on themselves.

"Go away Polly Fists!" she cried.

Then the phantom was gone.

Connie took three sharp breaths, then spun on her heels and raced back the way she had come. By the time she entered the meadow, Eddie had started searching for her. Relief washed through her. She hitched up her skirts and raced towards him. He ran to meet her, concern all over his face.

She would have flown into his arms, but for a distrusting mindset that caused her feet to slide to a stop just outside his reach.

They locked eyes. Standing so close, yet with an expanse between them that seemed impossible to cross. They searched behind each other's eyes, their breath quickening as they recognized a need in each other.

She was a conundrum he couldn't fathom. Part innocent, part sharp – part vulnerable, part strong. He experienced a driving urge to comfort and protect her, to afford her no sharp words and to draw her to him with every talent he possessed. In truth he was desperate to make her his own. He'd learned from a young boy that women's heads were easily turned by soft words, and that they rarely recognized flattery as disingenuous. He realized this woman before him was not impressed by words. With dawning clarity, he appreciated that she could be won over no other way than by actions. That only the passing of time would reveal to her, his motives and the measure of his true character.

She took a step forward.

He gulped. "I know you're lost right now, only grant me the chance to prove myself to you?"

She edged forward.

"I know I can promise you freedom, and a life beyond Devonshire, but unless you trust me and come with me, you'll never know if I'm a man of my word. You need to take a step of faith, Connie. Give me this chance, I beg of you."

One last step and now they were face to face. She raised a hand and laid the back of it against his cheek. His eyes closed. His chest rose and fell with quick succession as need to possess her coursed through his body. She tilted her face upwards; he felt the movement and opened his eyes. Hers were closed. Slowly so as not to scare her away, he leaned down and brushed his lips against hers. Connie's eyes flicked open and he pulled back.

"Woman, you are standing far too close for me to resist." Eddie's voice was low and husky; his breath caressed her face. She inhaled deeply and in that moment, she knew that this pirate was not her fisherman husband, who had always carried upon his person the stink of fish and the stale stench of booze.

"You need to take me, before thoughts of morality drag me away from you." Her purred demand set his whole being on fire. He grabbed her head with his hands and crashed his lips upon her once more. She moaned. Her surrender stole his heart. As he picked her up and tenderly carried her back into the woods, he swore to himself that he would spend every day of his life ensuring her happiness.

Chapter 15

"EDDIE?"

"Umm-mm."

"I still think someone is following us."

"I'm sure we escaped without being seen." He started looking behind them, searching everywhere.

"I'm not sure. I just have this odd feeling. It's the same one I used to have when Joseph was spying on me."

Eddie brought his gaze to her face.

"Is he haunting you?"

"Only his memory."

"And Polly?"

Connie didn't answer.

"Do you still see Polly?"

She didn't want him to leave her. "No, no."

After giving themselves to each other in the woods, Eddie had thought she would begin to trust him. He guessed she was lying, but until she was ready to be open with him, he wouldn't force it. They walked in comfortable silence for a while.

"Can you smell that?" asked Eddie sniffing the air.

"Bacon!"

"Hang caution to the wind, if we don't eat soon we won't make it to Modbury! Let's see if they are willing to offer us something." They picked up their pace until the smoke of a farmhouse chimney came into sight.

"Wait a moment." Eddie worked his way into the hedgerow and hid the chest under the soil there. Carefully, he covered the area with a sweep and made it look as if it had been undisturbed.

"You can't leave it there," said Connie.

"It'll be alright, we ain't seen a single soul since we started and it's well-hidden."

"Eddie you might not believe me, but I know someone is following us. I don't know who, but…"

"I'm sure Polly's ghost won't be able to dig up the chest."

"You're not listening to me! You said you would, you said you would always give me my voice and a vote. Well, I vote we don't leave it here. Someone is following us and it's not Polly!"

"We need something to eat, but you know what happened to us when we left the Cox's, who knows what a farmer with a gun might do if he thinks we 'ave treasure."

"You taint everyone with the same tar that is spread on you. Not everyone is a murdering thief."

"No, but some are. And let me tell you Connie Boyton… if you can look at a man and know what's in 'is heart, well you must have a connection to God, for sure as I live and breathe men who I thought good have surprised me."

"You stay hidden. I'll go and speak with whoever lives here."

Eddie shook his head. "No, if only one of us is to go, it should be me."

Connie sighed. "My accent will grant me quick access, while yours may result in a shut door."

Eddie thought about it for a while, and then relented. "Alright, but I'll stand behind the cow shed and be in hearing distance."

"Very well, it's agreed."

Connie walked up the main path and entered the farmyard in full view, while Eddie sneaked around the back and hid behind the shed. Someone must have seen her approach, for the door opened before she could knock.

"Well, bless my soul girl, what you doing here on your own?"

Connie looked up when she heard the voice and relief washed over her. "Sarah, you're a sight for sore eyes!"

The two of them embraced and promptly embarked upon quick chatter as only women can do. All sorts of questions poured from both of them, speaking at the same time.

"How are your parents? How are the vicar and his wife?"

"How long have you lived here? I thought you had gone to Cornwall; that was the rumor anyway."

The two of them paused and then broke out laughing.

"Come on inside, Constance. Let us exchange our news in comfort."

"I'd love to, but I'm not alone. Can my… friend… enter as well?"

The busty farmwife raised one eyebrow. "If he's a friend of yours, then he'll be welcome."

"Thank you." Connie turned around and cupped her hands over her mouth. "Eddie, come on out."

"No need to shout woman," said Eddie who immediately popped from around the side of the farmhouse wall.

"Good Lord!" cried the farmwife who had nearly jumped out of her skin.

"Excuse me," said Eddie with a cheeky grin.

"This is Sarah, her family used to own the farm next to ours when we were growing up. She disappeared one day, her folks said she gone to get married, but because she didn't say goodbye to anyone we all guessed she'd run away."

"Yep that I did… but only as far as Ermington, and all to marry the youngest son of a farmer with a reputation for gambling and womanizing. My folks were so horrified at my choice that they shut the door on me, God bless their souls. Now come on in before there is no food left, for my Bert he does like a good portion." She chuckled to herself as she led them in.

The farmhouse was old but in its day had been grand. The kitchen offered a wide space for all manner of farm tasks, and sitting proudly in the center was a long oak table that had been there for thirty years. It was homely and fresh. The smells floating around the room, made both Eddie and Connie's stomachs rumble loudly, which caused both Sarah and Bert and their four sons to laugh.

"Sit down, sit down," said Bert. "Oscar and Steven give up your seats now." The two youngsters jumped up straight away.

"Thank you," said both Eddie and Connie sitting down next to each other.

For the next hour, the talk was merry. Much reminiscing was exchanged between the two women.

Eventually, Eddy asked a question that had been bothering him since their arrival. Addressing Sarah, he said, "You mentioned Ermington before?"

"Yes, that's right."

"Is that to say, that is where we are?"

"It is indeed," chipped in Bert, "well unless some trickster has gone and upped us and moved us without our knowing!" To which his family all laughed heartily.

"Then we are close to the village of Modbury?"

"We are somewhat, although the town of Ermington is much closer. If you want Modbury you will need to head southeast out of here, go up our pathway, turn right, go to the crossroads and after that follow the stone marking to Modbury. It's three miles at most."

"What will you do there?" asked Sarah.

"We've been told there's a man there who sells horses."

"Oh, you'll mean old Parry Eldon, I'm afraid you're out of luck. Old Parry died this winter gone. If you're looking to buy a horse, you'll need to fetch yourselves to Ivybridge. Be a few folk there who deal with the beasts. Afraid you won't have much luck around here."

"I don't suppose you have one you could sell us, even an old nag or a small pony? I have coin and can pay you over the price so you can buy yourself another when you have the opportunity."

Bert shook his head. "Would if I could, and the extra coin would be much welcomed, but alas, we've not had a horse for a time now. Times are mighty hard, we're holding on to the farm by the skin of our teeth and that's the truth."

After breakfast a flurry of activity followed, in which they exchanged gifts. A parcel of food wrapped in a clean cloth, one of Sarah's best skirts so that Connie could give Eddie his belt back, and a pair of ankle boots that Sarah kept for best fitted Connie's feet well enough, though they were slightly loose.

"This doubloon is too much!" gasped Sarah when they gave it to her.

"Oh please accept it and do what you will with it, hopefully it will help tide you over until a good harvest comes in," said Connie who had secretly left another one under Sarah's pillow while she changed her skirt. She would have left the lot, but Eddie whisked the chest out of her reach when he saw the second one being taken. A sack bag was given for Eddie to put the chest in so that he could carry it on his back, and... after much persuasion, Bert handed Eddie a fine dagger.

"Not been used since my grandfather's day, but I will miss it."

"Then we should leave it with you!" said Connie, trying to wrestle it out of Eddie's hands.

Bert put a hand on Connie's arm. "Nay lass, it's fine, let your man keep it. The coin you have given is worth a hundred daggers and that's for sure."

They left the farm better equipped for their journey and content now their stomachs were full. Sarah waved to them as they left.

"She was always a rum 'un," said Connie. "My ma was always cross when I spent time with her, but she came out good and seems happy with her lot in life."

The day had raced away from them, and the sun had tipped its peak a while gone as they set off down the road. The day was sunny and warm, and when Connie slipped her hand into Eddie's, a sense of well-being came over him.

Chapter 16

WALKING SOON BECOMES wearisome when forced to foot the byways for such long periods of time, and Connie longed for it to end. This march into an unknown future was not the stuff of her daydreams and she began to long for a carriage to carry them to Liverpool. Eddie had started getting edgy, and she wondered if he too, was at last, feeling the presence of eyes of on their backs. He took them off the road and decided a footpath would be a much safer track for them.

It was growing dark when they unexpectedly came upon a ruined manor house. The building had obviously once been grand, with its two floors and many windows. No lights shone through the windows and there was no sound except for a whistling wind that spun a rooster-shaped weather vane around and around.

It was a rambling old house in a state of total disrepair. Ivy had covered the left side of the building seemingly making the house fade in and mingle with the overgrowth of many trees and bushes.

"Do you think it's empty?" asked Eddie.

"Surely it must be," Connie whispered back.

Nevertheless, they approached cautiously, their feet scrunching through a mixture of shingle (that must have formed the old road), and years of dried grasses and leaves.

"What a shame," said Connie as they approached the door, "I can imagine it was once a proud home."

Eddie pushed the door, it didn't move. He looked at Connie and shrugged before lifting up his hand and knocking loudly upon it. They waited a while but no response came.

"Let's look around the back; maybe a kitchen door remains unlocked."

When they came to the back, they were surprised to find it in much better condition than the front of the house. It looked like a kitchen garden was still in use, and most surprisingly a neigh sounded from the stable.

Eddie's eyes lit up, and he rushed to open the stable door. Sure enough inside was a horse, though it looked worse for wear; old, with a mottled mane and a sore eye. "Hello, old girl, you've seen better days now haven't you?" The horse nuzzled against Eddie's hands. Eddie chuckled, "Now aren't you the easy one!"

"I didn't know you were good with horses," said Connie watching him with a smile.

"Not just horses, all animals."

Connie thought of a memory of her father when he had told her you could always gauge a good man by how well he treated animals. The memory made her smile as she watched Eddie rub his head into the horse's neck.

"Well," he said turning to look at her. "Obviously the house isn't as deserted as we thought. Let's take the horse and be gone."

"We can't do that!"

"Yes, we can." Eddie made to open the half-barn door to let the animal out into the stable, while his eyes searched the shelves for a saddle.

Connie put a hand on his arm. "I won't do it."

Eddie simply stared at her, his chin squared and his brow lowered. "Your feet will be ruined before we reach Liverpool."

"I don't care. Either we go to the house and ask to buy it, or we continue on foot."

Still in need of proving himself a changed man, Eddie agreed. The door to the kitchen was ajar. Eddie knocked on it. When no response came, he pushed it wide. Warily, they stepped inside. The kitchen was untidy, but there were obvious signs it was still in use, and recently for when Eddie touched the pan sitting on the table, it was still lukewarm.

"Helloooo!" called Connie.

They moved from the kitchen to the grand hallway.

"Villains!" An apparition of in white flung itself across the room and launched his hands towards Eddie's throat. "What sayest thou?" cried the old man seized by the energy produced by the tempest of rage. With trembling hands, thin and spindly, he did shake an astonished Eddie by the collar.

"We mean you no 'arm, good sire," stammered Eddie, while disengaging himself from the man as carefully as possible so as not to hurt him.

"We have entered your home unbidden, only to pay you for your old nag," added Connie hovering to the side, not knowing what to do.

"Pay me?" the man dropped his arms and looked confused. "Pay me?" he repeated as he walked across the room and perched on the end of a threadbare sofa.

Eddie and Connie walked over to him.

"Does someone live here with you? Is there someone we can call to aid you?" asked Connie.

"No one but me in these walls for over thirty years. All gone. All gone, every last one of them... all gone." The old chap dropped his chin to his chest, forcing his tall nightcap to wobble. He sat before them in bare feet wearing a long, grayish-white nightshirt.

Eddie and Connie looked at each other not sure what to do.

"We can't stay," said Eddie, and Connie knew the truth of it.

"Can we buy your old nag?" she asked the man, leaning down to be level with his face.

"My Annabelle is a thoroughbred; she'd be too expensive for the likes of you!"

"She's a beauty," said Eddie, "but she ain't 'alf old, she's not worth much these days I'm afraid."

"Then you won't want her," the man said, suddenly appearing extremely alert and canny.

"I'll give you eighteen guineas for her," said Eddie.

"And who will keep me company when my old girl is gone, eh, I ask you that?"

"Does no one visit you?" asked Connie.

"Told you," snapped the man, "there's no one left but me."

"Come on," said Connie tugging on Eddie's sleeve. "Let's go." Her 'eerie' feeling was back, prickles ran down her back as she tried to shrug off the impression someone was spying on them again.

Eddie heard the slight tremor in her voice. "Again?"

She nodded.

"Maybe we should stay the night 'ere?"

"Oh no," cried Connie. "We need to go, we really do."

"You can sleep in the barn if you like," offered the old man. "Probably drier than the rooms upstairs anyway, roof's been going for years. Leaking it is, like a sieve."

"No. Thank you, but no. Eddie we have to go!"

For a moment Eddie wondered what he had taken on by falling in love with a woman that saw ghosts and constantly felt watched and threatened. But he didn't like the fear in her eyes and wanted her peace.

"It's a long way to the next village, you sure you don't want to stay in the barn and we'll set off at first light?" he asked.

She didn't have to say no. The color had drained from her face and her eyes had grown large and frozen. He turned around to see what she was looking at. Nothing.

Connie's chest was rising and falling, her breath tiny rapid gasps. He took her hand. "Come on, we'll go now."

She wouldn't budge and he was about to start imploring her when he noticed the trickle of tears rolling from the corner of her eye. He picked her up and swung her into his arms. Connie rolled her head into his chest and started sobbing.

He knew whatever it was she was seeing was wearing her down and making her senses weaker. As they went from the hallway into the kitchen, the old man, whose name they'd never asked, cried out, "Leave the money on the table!"

Eddie smiled. The nag wasn't much, but he could put Connie on its back and he could run beside them. They would get to Liverpool much quicker now. He popped Connie down while he put his hands into the sack to get a coin from the chest. Connie started shaking violently. He put a gold doubloon on the table, it was miles too much but he had no guineas and wasn't inclined to ask the old chap for change, he probably wouldn't have it anyway. If they kept on like this the chest would soon be empty, but this new generous side to him gave him a warm feeling. Who knew that helping people felt so good? He picked Connie up again, who still stood trembling where he'd put her, she instantly burrowed into his chest.

"Lord, what am I do to with you?" he murmured as he felt her shaking.

Standing by the kitchen door was the image of Polly. Again she looked to be trying to say something, but her lips appeared locked together by some unnatural force. Polly kept turning her head towards the door, then looking back at Connie, and if a bland-white face could look afraid, hers did.

Connie began to shake violently. Eddie wanted to see her face and so placed her down in a chair. "What's happening, my girl?"

Polly screamed! Her mouth still closed, but the shrill that filled the house had most definitely come from her. Eddie froze.

Tightening his arms around Connie, he whispered, "Was that her?"

Connie nodded. Then in a split-second, Polly was gone, and the way was clear for them to leave.

"What was that noise?" croaked the old man shuffling into the kitchen. Spotting the gold on the table, he nearly choked.

"An early night owl, I should think," answered Eddie.

"Owl my foot," said the man. He scowled at Connie. "You're not leaving me your friend here are you?"

"Friend?" asked Eddie.

"Uh-huh, her dead friend she lugs around with her. You leave her with me and I will curse you to hell, and that is a promise!"

Eddie didn't know what to think as he slowly turned his head around to look all around the kitchen. He couldn't see anything.

"She's gone," whimpered Connie.

"And best not be coming back," snapped the old man as he snatched the coin off the table and held it behind his back.

"Connie?" Eddie still didn't know what to do.

"Let's go," she pleaded.

No sooner were they out of the kitchen, than they heard the old man putting a bolt in place. "No refunds!" he yelled at them through the door.

"Do you want me to carry you?"

She shook her head.

They walked the short distance to the stable, and Eddie set to work saddling the old nag. As he tied his bag to the saddle, he momentarily had his back to Connie.

She screamed.

Eddie swung around to a sight he had not been expecting.

Holding Connie tightly against him and pressing a knife at her throat was none other than Hawk-Eye, Captain Harry Hawkins.

"Hello me old matey," sneered Hawkins.

For a split-second, the sight of the supposedly dead pirate froze him. Then Eddie lurched forward, "Get yer hands off her!"

Connie yelped and cried in pain as the knife cut into her neck.

"Whoa, whoa, Earnest Eddie, steady yourself, don't be stupid, or your foxy lady here will be no more."

Eddie wavered, trying to work out the best plan of attack.

"If you come for me, she's a dead 'un, Eddie. On that you have my word."

Eddie knew how easily Hawkins took life, and so stayed his hand and tried to remain still.

"There's a good boy. Now here's what's going to happen. You're going to bring that horse to me. I'm going to take it and your floozy here, and when I'm a short bit away, I'll climb into the saddle and let this one go. If you try to stop me, you have my word I'll kill her. What say you, boatswain?"

What could he do? Eddie nodded.

"I need the words boy!"

Eddie ground his teeth. "You 'ave my word I'll not jump you, just don't hurt her."

Eddie led the horse into the stable yard. Hawkins kept the knife at Connie's throat. They moved together keeping a steady distance.

"You'll be alright," Eddie told her. "He has no reason to kill you."

Hawkins took the reins in one hand, keeping Connie pressed to him by the pressure of the knife. He walked backwards towards the hole in the stone wall; the gate which had long perished lay on the ground beside it. They passed through the gap and Hawkins judged it a safe distance. He laughed.

"When have you ever known me to keep my word, Calstock?"

"No!" yelled Eddie and darted towards them.

Connie felt the pressure increase and knew Hawkins was about to slit her throat.

In that very moment… a roar came from the hedge behind the gardens. A large, black shadow flung itself across the way and landed on the back of Hawkins.

Hawkins nipped Connie's neck as he fell to the floor.

She dropped to her knees and pressed her hands to her neck.

Eddie charged with Bert's dagger in his hand.

The shadow yelled, "Stop Earnest Eddie!" and put a hand up towards him.

"Sam?" said Eddie, "good Lord, you made it!"

Sam Mountain grinned and displayed a row of brilliant white teeth. "The Gods don't want me yet," he laughed.

"Let me kill him," said Eddie.

Sam was kneeling on Hawkins' chest and held the captain's hands pinned over his head with one hand, while his other hand picked up the dropped dagger and waved it at Eddie to bid him to stop where he was.

"You stole from us, Earnest Eddie."

Eddie blanched and would have paled if he had any color left in his cheeks. "I planned to share it with the survivors."

"Well, we're survivors," squeaked Hawkins, glaring through his one good eye.

"Our crew would still be 'ere, if you 'ad listened to me," snapped Eddie.

"The past is gone, nought to be done about it now. I regret not turning for shore when you said, and I'm sorry for it. Sam, why not get off me now, eh?"

Sam moved off him, but he kept hold of Hawkins' knife.

"Three-way share it is then," said Hawkins standing up and brushing his skinny body down.

Eddie noticed his state for the first time, pitiful he looked, like a man close to death. "What happened to you?"

"Smiley did for me, he did. Captured me and Fontana off the beach, fished us out like we were nothing but sardines. Fontana told him that he'd seen you with the chest and that was the end of him, Smiley slit his throat and gloated about it to me. After that he spent days trying to find out if we had hidden plunder anywhere. He said he'd heard rumors that we had the largest haul of treasure any pirate had ever seen."

Eddie stiffened.

"Don't worry, I told him all we had was in that small chest," Hawkins laughed, but the sound held no merriment in it.

Eddie felt Connie looking at him, but wouldn't return her glance.

"There's no treasure, Connie, the chest is all there is."

Hawkins laughed again, looking at Connie with a look that told her she would be stupid to believe him.

"How did you escape from Smiley?" asked Sam Mountain.

"Well now if that wasn't the darndest thing! Smiley had only gone and hooked himself up with my sister now hadn't he!"

"Polly?" said Connie with a croak. She'd ripped a piece of her skirt when the talking had begun and tied it around her neck. The scratch had stopped bleeding, but she wanted to keep it clean.

"Yeah, I'd not seen her since we were thirteen. The last thing I did before I scarpered for the seas was to rescue her from a brute. So, when she brought me some water I claimed what was due and demanded she set me free."

"And she did?" asked Connie.

"Course she did, blood is thicker than water now ain't it!"

"Polly set you free…"

"She did, I said that already."

"And Smiley killed her for it," trilled Connie with a squeak.

"That ain't my fault, I told her I did, to run with me. But she wouldn't do it, mumbled something about him being the only man she'd ever loved and after sneaking me along the beach and taking me inland a bit, she went back."

"And he killed her." Fire was burning inside Connie. She wanted to take the dagger from Eddie and stab this weasel with it. "And you've been following me, us, ever since."

Hawkins sneered. "I was hiding when I heard you coming, lying low in the bracken. It was easy to lose Smiley's men in all that long grass. There I was hiding away, when you rushed by all soaking wet. And I wondered to myself… what can a pretty young thing like that be doing out at such a time. So I followed you to see what you were up to. Hark at my surprise when you led me straight to Calstock! I thought to myself… well ain't my stars blessed, first my long-lost sister and now the stealing boatswain given to me like gifts."

"And you Sam, how long 'ave you been following us?" asked Eddie, realizing now that Connie had been right all along.

"Since the first day. I saw her and her friend," he tipped his forehead towards Connie, "take you off the beach and so I followed."

"All this time," said Eddie, and now sadness had fallen over his face. "Why didn't you come forward? We could have done this adventure together."

"I didn't know how things would play out, Eddie. At first, I knew you didn't have the treasure for I checked in on you that first night, when you were dead to the world. After that I wasn't sure what to do. I decided to wait and see how the wind blew. And here we all are."

"I wish you 'ad been friend enough to come forward Sam, but I'll admit I'm more than grateful that you saved Connie's life. I'm in your debt."

"We are equal Earnest Eddie, no debt is due, you saved my life and now I've saved the life of your woman."

Eddie turned back to Hawkins. "Why did you wait till now to come forward?"

"Truth is I lost you that night you legged it. I wandered around not knowing where to go. Then blow me down with a feather, but didn't you go and come back! I watched you get the chest and I've been waiting for my moment ever since. As soon as I saw you saddling the horse, I thought to myself it's now or never, 'cos once you ride off that will be that. Let us divvy up the gold and be on our separate ways," said Hawkins. "Into four parts that is, one each for you two, and two parts for me; seeing as how I was the captain."

"No," said Eddie, Sam and Connie together.

All of them looked at Connie.

"This ain't none of your business wench!" snarled Hawkins.

"We will split it into three," said Eddie, "equal parts each."

"No!" said Connie.

"Woman you test me," snarled Hawkins.

"This is the right thing to do, Connie. We all agreed to the Commonwealth Agreement for Pirates, we can't go back on our bond now."

"I found the gold. I kept the gold hidden from Smiley, even though he and his crew searched every inch of the coast for it.

It's mine by rights, I demand my equal share and if you can't agree on that, I'll keep it all!"

Eddie burst out laughing, and Sam grinned from ear to ear.

"You're not going along with that?" screeched Hawkins.

"Seems right to me," said Sam Mountain.

"And me," said Eddie.

Despite Hawkins' constant moans, Eddie split the coins into four equal piles and counted out thirty to each of them. Hawkins and Sam filled their pockets; Connie kept hers in her cupped hands.

"If I see you again, Hawkins, I will run you through," said Eddie.

"Farewell to you too," called Hawkins already backing away before the others could change their mind and steal his share.

They watched him until he disappeared into the night.

"Stay with us Sam," said Eddie.

"Where do you head?" asked Sam.

"To Liverpool, and from there a ship for the Americas and a new life. We have big dreams, Sam. We are to buy land and start farming, come with us, it will be a good life."

"Not for the likes of me," replied Sam.

"You would be part of our family," said Connie. "I owe you my life and I would do all I can to make sure you always felt like you were surrounded by family. Come with us."

Sam smiled. "Thank you kindly, mam, but I must make my own path. But listen Eddie, don't go to Liverpool."

"Why's that?"

"I spent many a night outside tavern windows; you learn things listening to private conversations. I've heard that ships sail from Plymouth for a place called Pen-nsyl-van-ia, if that's the right way to say it. The Whigs want rid of people they call 'Poor Palatines' and are encouraging them to leave England for the Americas. They've been promised free transportation and free land when they arrive. Pretend you to be these people and get your free ship and land! You just have to profess to be good, foreign Protestants! If you know who they are?"

Connie and Eddie looked at each other. Was this a gift? Was it a sign that there might be a future out there for them that wasn't crippled by bad luck?

"Thank you, Sam. We'll think on it." Sam and Eddie gripped elbows and pulled each other's arm. "I wish you would come with us, Sam."

"I don't think I look like a Protestant!" laughed Sam.

"Take care of Earnest Eddie for me, mam. He's rough around the edges but you know his heart is good, and with a man like that you can't go wrong."

Connie smiled. "Thank you Sam, I'll do my best."

After he was gone, Connie and Eddie looked at other, but before they could say anything, a white apparition appeared behind them.

This time it was only the old man from the house. "I thought they'd never go," he said announcing his presence. "Well if it's good Protestants you want to be, you'd best spend the night in the barn. Come to the kitchen in the morning, we'll break our fast together and I'll tell you as much as I can, also I have a King James you can have, for I'm sure no good Protestant would travel without one."

Without waiting for an answer, he turned and went back into the house.

Connie and Eddie laughed, and for the first time since they'd met it was a joyous, carefree laugh.

Chapter 17

WHAT HAD SHE BECOME? A murderer and friend of pirates – how could that have happened? Why had she let it happen? What foolish woman rescues a pirate and expects to carry on her life as normal? Polly had been right about her, for she'd held in her core a longing for Eddie to rescue her, but she'd never thought that meant her husband's murder – and at her own hands! She was doomed to hell!

Last night Eddie had professed his love for her, in between acts that in all senses except church, made her his wife. Although she hadn't said the words back to him, she had a growing suspicion that she loved him. Whether that blossoming love stemmed from something real, or whether her need to escape and her longing for someone to take care of her persuaded her she was in love, she couldn't tell.

Eddie had fallen asleep quickly, while Connie could not turn her thoughts off and so had remained awake most of the night. The morning approached now, and she lay on her side and gazed into his ruggedly handsome face. Watching Eddie sleeping, she pondered on the error of her ways and it twisted her insides tightly. Bad blood… who can change when their blood is bad? It always shows its true colors in the end, there's no denying it. She had gone from the frying pan into the fire. She'd pushed her husband over a cliff and was now on the run with a pirate with a ruthless reputation. She was crazy! Dragged into the current of self-pity, Connie felt helpless to extricate herself from blame. She deserved prison or worse, and would confess all to the first man of the law she met.

Her dream of freedom had become even more impossible now; she would never be free again. Even if somehow she evaded the gallows, she would always carry the vision of Joseph's face as he went over the cliff. More precisely, she recalled the joy that had surged through her when she pushed him, she was a thoroughly wicked woman and deserving of punishment. If that wasn't enough, the guilt of Polly drew the poor pirate's spirit along with her wherever she went. If the judge could see her self-inflicted punishment, he would send her on her way and say, 'surely you are punished enough.'

She might be free now of beatings and bruises, but they had been replaced with something far worse (Polly had been right about that too) for remorse was more painful than anything she'd ever felt.

Images of things she had once considered trivial popped into her mind: gossip amongst neighbors; church on Sundays; going to market once a week or bouncing babies upon hips. Such activities produced a measure of pleasure and contentment for others. But Connie had never been a part of the trivialities of a normal life. She was a loner, content only in her own company. Enjoying the absence of idle chit-chat was her pastime, the sound of nature the language of her choice. She considered herself past the age of possible change.

With emotions out of control, suffocation suddenly overcame her. Panic stole her breath. Her hands fluttered before her chest, which rose and fell in dramatic heaves.

Eddie stirred. "What is it? What's wrong?" Eddie endeavored to comfort her and wrapped his arms around her. To Connie, his arms felt like heavy, heavy chains, pinning her down to a life she did not want.

She opened her mouth, but no sound came out.

Eddie realized at once that her body had gone stiff under his embrace and removed his arms immediately. When her breathing had eased somewhat, he placed a tentative hand on her knee. With his glance he implored her to confide in him. "I can't begin to imagine what you are suffering, but Connie, you need to hear me. I am for you. Never will I be against you. If you decide you do not want to remain by my side I will abide by your wishes. I will take you wherever you want to go. I will see you settled and provided for somehow and I will leave you to live the life you chose. Do you understand? I will never force my will upon you. You are a free woman."

In her mind she was screaming… 'I will never be free!' The past was already building a gilded cage around her from which she would never escape. But she wanted to live; whether that was with Eddie or alone she had yet to make her decision. She pulled at the cloth around her neck until it came loose. It revealed a long, thin angry cut. "We will need honey," she said.

"Then let us go and see if the old man is up, after which we'll be on our way." In his mind he asked, but to where?

Not only was the squire up but eggs were in the pan.

They broke their fast with him as he rambled on about all he knew about Protestants. He had no honey, but assured them the next town would have plenty. They accepted the Bible gratefully and promised to take good care of it.

"Will you be alright?" Connie asked as they were leaving.

"There's life in my old bones yet, don't you worry."

With Annabelle fed and saddled once more, Connie climbed into the saddle.

"You look after my old girl, find her a good home when you get to Plymouth, promise me that. Don't let her end up in the knackers' yard."

"I'll find her a good home," said Eddie, touched to see the old man had watery eyes.

"Remember… road to Yealmpton, then Brixton, and then on for the ferry in Turnchapel. That way you'll be taken straight to the port and you will miss a lot of travelers on the main road. Too many nosy people about these days; can't be too careful."

"We'll remember," said Connie. She waved for a long time as they set off, until the old squire finally turned around and went inside.

They went on their way with a certain lightness in their spirit. Eddie especially was full of optimism, Connie not so much as she wrestled with her woes. As it happened, Annabelle was well past her days of traveling far, and kept stopping to eat grass.

"Blasted animal," cursed Eddie when once again she refused to raise her head from the ground.

Connie got the giggles, and slid off the saddle to help try and coax the old horse along. "We'll have to give her away as soon as we find her a home."

"Waste of good money," moaned Eddie.

"To be fair, the old man didn't ask you to pay him a gold doubloon."

Eddie didn't answer.

Eventually, Annabelle raised her head and allowed Eddie to lead her on.

"You getting back on?" asked Eddie.

"No, I'll walk a little, we might go faster!" They laughed, what else could they do.

After a while, Eddie asked, "Do you not love me Connie?"

"I guess a little, otherwise I would have taken my share and been gone wouldn't I?"

"I thought you wanted none of the money?"

"I changed my mind after you left the squire a coin. First, you gave one to Sarah and Bert and then you gave one to him. I realized that the coins may have been ill-gained, but they can be used for good."

"So that's what you're going to do, give it all away?"

"I plan to."

"Who to?"

"I don't know yet, do I? But when I come across someone needy, I will know."

"Noble cause."

"You could do the same?"

"Robin Hood, me? I don't think so!"

They walked along for a while lost in their own thoughts.

"Do you think they've found Joseph's body?" asked Connie.

"Yes."

"And you think they'll know it was me? They won't assume it was an accident?"

"I don't think so Connie, but you never know. They won't know where you are so they might assume you killed him and ran away. But what has occurred to me these last few hours is that the whole village is caught up in smuggling so they won't want any attention from the magistrates. They might claim it as an accident to keep the law away."

Connie looked at him as they walked. "Really?"

"It's what I would do… would have done, and Smiley won't want anyone snooping around Burr Island, that's for sure."

"I might be clear of trouble?"

Eddie stopped walking and looked at her, face on.

"You need to remember that you were only protecting yourself. But now I think on it, I'm sure you have nothing to worry about. You're free, Connie, free as a bird and you can go wherever you wish."

Free as a bird, oh how she had dreamed of this day. Maybe things would work out after all.

"Give us a kiss," she said. Eddie needed no second asking. He pulled her against his chest with his strong arms and smothered her face with kisses. "My lips, my lips," she laughed, kiss me on my lips!"

Yealmpton was the biggest place Connie had ever been in her life. It was a bustle of activity and her senses tingled with excitement. They made inquiries and then headed for the Lyneham Inn to seek lodging for the night.

It was a staunch looking building, nothing at all like the petite inns in Bigbury-on-Sea or even the comfortable Cox's. It appeared like a large square block. Made from dull stone bricks, with a gray slate roof, it had no charm about it.

The innkeeper was sweeping the floors to add fresh straw as they entered. He looked up and seemed somehow weary. "Well met, how may I serve you today?"

"Good sir, I'm in need of a room for myself and my wife, and a meal if you're serving?"

"Aye, can offer you both. Come along in."

Although it was spring, and a large fire burned merrily in the hearth, there was an indifferent and cool atmosphere to the place, and Connie decided it was too large for her.

"It's just for one night," Eddie whispered to her when she grimaced.

"Good sir, we 'ave tied to your fence a very old nag that we 'ave no more need for. Do you know of a family that has children? We think they might enjoy learning to ride on such a gentle old beast."

"Well knock me down! My Bertha did ask for a horse only the other day, and I said to her… well no, my sweet pea, we have no money to buy such a beast. And here you are offering a horse for free! What providence!"

"She's very old," added Connie, "but gentle and mild in nature and perfect we think for a child."

"Well then I'll be glad to take her off your hands."

"Her name is Annabelle."

"I'll show you your room first and tend to her after. Come this way. You've come at the busiest time of the month," the innkeeper said as he led them down a corridor.

"Why's that?" asked Connie.

"It be market day today, it's always on the fourth Wednesday of each month and today is that day."

"Arr, so that's why it's busy," said Eddie.

"Yep, that's right, be quiet as a graveyard again tomorrow. And this new turnpike is largely to blame. Why they built this toll pike right 'ere, is beyond me. Local folk been up in arms about it they have. You know the toll be 1d. for a horse, 3d. for a carriage, and 6d. for a cart! Can you believe the robbery of it! Folk have been up to the Lyneham Estate to complain to his nibs himself. Daylight robbery it is, a grievous tax upon our freedom of movement from place to place and so we all say! And the road's still a mess to boot!"

"I understand your pain," said Eddie.

"Well here you are, you freshen up and come back for a bite of supper when you're ready. Nothing grand, but wholesome and filling."

"Thank you, we'll be down presently."

They listened to his steps as he retreated to the main room and then fell to laughing.

"He didn't even question that we were married, you're truly a wicked person Eddie Calstock!"

"Oh Connie, do you not feel a burden lifted? You're a widow in truth and entitled to remarry without breaking any laws or committing a sin. Let's marry and when I introduce you as my wife you'll not think so badly of me."

"A woman who murdered her husband and a pirate who has murdered many, I'm not so sure I'll ever stop thinking badly of you or me."

"Oh for a little while be merry! Let us eat and drink and enjoy our time together. Both of us know that life is short and we'll never know when calamity will strike at us again. Let's live and make hay while the sun shines!"

The bustle of excitement danced like fireflies betwixt them. The air was alive and infectious and Connie drowned in the intoxicating attraction. She suddenly yearned for things she'd previously considered impossible. A tender touch, a warm strong embrace, a kiss. Oh a kiss from those full and inviting lips! Her eyes feasted where her thoughts dwelled, and so his smile was caught and forever impressed upon her mind. Such a smile! Such lips!

Then the item of her attention swung forward and fell gently upon her own. At first, soft and inquiring, then immediately blazing to hard, demanding and yet... giving. A kiss to entice angels down from Heaven. Every part of her melted, his arms snaked around her body and pulled her to him. She lost her breath and became light-headed. He moved from her lips to her cheek and then her neck. She moaned, and would have sunk further into his being if it were possible.

At last, he pulled away from her, his breathing deep, his eyes bloodshot and fired with deep longing. "You had best marry me, my girl, so I can make an honest woman of you."

Too used to being obedient she almost said yes, but then she pulled back. It took strength to tear away her gaze from his eyes and turn away, but she did. "I will not be forced!" She was out through the door and running before Eddie knew what was going on. Back through the inn and out into the early evening. She headed away from the village and towards the fields. Racing away from the flare of need and desire that had cracked open her carefully hardened heart. The spin of emotions drowned her. She fought ferociously to bury them again. Love equaled pain and she wanted none of it. Desiring happiness brought nothing but sorrow and she would *not* go there! The equilibrium of her life came with complete lack of emotions. She would not give up her control... or peace, for a useless dream. It was an illusion that, when pulled back, presented nothing but sorrow. Yet... as she ran, his eyes bore a hole in her heart, for in truth her desire had mirrored his.

Chapter 18

CONNIE DIDN'T RETURN TO THE INN. She knew Eddie would be worried when she stayed away all night, but she needed a moment to herself. There was so much to digest, to break down and understand about what had happened. Whenever Connie closed her eyes, she saw the dead walking around, lost and searching for rest. Joseph, Polly and the men she had been unable to avert her eyes from on the beach. Her own bumps and bruises she found easy to ignore, while plastering her face with indifference. But the death of Polly, Joseph and the pirates would not allow her to remain placid, buried emotions kept defying her every effort and rose to choke her at any time that took their fancy.

The coldest hour, just before sunrise, surged through the ground with an icy touch, which caused her skin to hurt. Denied sound sleep for yet another night, the turn of the day found her weakened and lacking energy. She rose from her spot on the edge of a farmed field and stretched. About to set off for the inn, a thought caused her to halt and stand still. Polly! From the moment Hawkins had left them at the old manor, she had never seen Polly again. As clear as day she suddenly understood it all. Polly hadn't been haunting her, she had been trying to warn her about her brother! Did that mean that Polly didn't blame her after all? The more she dwelled on what Hawkins had said about Polly rescuing him, the more she thought it was likely that

Smiley had killed her for that reason. She wasn't to blame! But Joseph... the memory of his hands squeezing her neck, drew her hands there. There was no doubt that he had been trying to kill her. She recalled the look of murder in his eyes and shivered. Eddie was right, of course he was, she'd only been protecting herself.

Eddie, she had to tell Eddie! She ran as fast as she could back to the Lyneham Inn. A pale light was emerging with the promise of a new day, and Connie's heart soared with the hope of a new life. She hesitated outside the inn's entrance, knowing it would no doubt be locked. As she stood there the door opened. One look at his drained face and Connie knew that Eddie had waited by the window for her and had also gone a night without sleep. She flew into his arms, and he crushed her body against his. Keeping one arm wrapped around her, he guided her inside and led her to their room. Excitedly she shared her revelations with him. As she talked, he untied her laces and helped her out of her damp, cold clothes. He led her to the bed, tucked the blankets around her, and then placed her skirts and blouse on different things as close to the low-burning fire as he could get them. After stripping off his clothes and with a relieved sigh, he climbed into bed with her.

"Don't you think it's marvelous that Polly has gone?" she asked.

He kissed her on the forehead. "I really do. Now let us sleep for a few hours, for we still have a journey before us."

"Oh I don't think I could sleep!"

"But I must, so maybe, if you're willing, I could hold you while I sleep a little while?"

She snuggled into him and wrapped her arm around his warm, hairy chest. "Like this?" she asked.

"Yes, just like that."

Eddie was feeling the exhaustion of stress brought on by worry. His eyelids closed instantly, but Connie's little snorts and heavy breathing let him know that she had fallen asleep quicker than he could say Jack Rabbit!

Eddie woke with Connie's moaning. "Shush," he murmured and stroked her hair. But the dream was as violent as a venomous snake, its hiss and devilish slither around Polly's lifeless body was more than Connie could take, and she woke with a scream on her lips.

He wrapped his arms around her. "I'm here, I'm here. It's alright, I'm here."

For a moment she looked at him confused, and then sobbing she threw herself against his chest. He let her cry. The sorrow of loss needed an outlet and tears were greatly overdue after he had previously cut them short.

"Why is life so terrible?" said Connie as she finally pushed herself away from his comforting and sat up.

"Polly?"

"No, it was the pirates – your crew that haunted me. Their deaths seemed so monstrous and I felt helpless to do anything about it. I don't think I shall ever forget their faces."

"Maybe with time…"

"Maybe."

Eddie requested some warm water and soap, and after they had washed and dressed they made their way to the lounge for something to eat, it was almost lunchtime by the time they had a meal.

"You remember what roads to take to go the quickest way?" asked the landlord for about the third time.

"Keep west as the crow flies, go straight and don't meander and in three hours at the most we'll be in Turnchapel."

"You sure you don't want to wait here for the next stagecoach? Would save your feet and that's for sure."

"We're ready to go now, and on foot is fine, please don't worry yourself," said Connie.

"The path to Brixton is straight and flat, you'll be there is less than an hour. Make sure to ask someone there to put you on the right path after that for there are a few farm lanes around there and if you take the wrong one you'll be walking a lot longer than you want."

"We'll do that, thank you good sir for your warm hospitality," said Eddie.

The innkeeper beamed, "'Tis my pleasure! Be sure to stop in at Old Mother Hubbard's cottage on the way out of the village. I've told her about you and she wants to give you a gift."

"That is too sweet of her, but we are not in need of gifts," said Connie.

"Just be sure to stop or you'll disappoint her. She's a retired housekeeper from Kitley Manor and is always busy. I told her of your generous gift of the horse to my daughter, and as she is like a grandmother to our Becky, well she wants to give you her thanks. You can't miss her cottage, it's built from old stones and well whitewashed, it has an extensive sweeping thatch that sits on it like an old wig, ha-ha. Anyway, you won't miss it; she'll probably be swinging in her rocking chair outside the door waiting for you. Farewell to you now, and safe journey."

Sure enough, an old woman was rocking in her chair, which she left in a hurry as soon as she spotted them walking down the lane.

"I have something for 'ee," said the rosy-cheeked woman.

"There's no need for a gift," said Eddie straight away.

"Nay laddie, you can't deny me the chance of a blessing. I have a tweed shawl for your good wife. The colors are dull, the dye's not been bright for a while, but the tweed is soft and mighty warm. Here," she held out the folded shawl to Connie.

"Thank you," said Connie raising the cloth to her cheek. "It's so soft, I will treasure it, thank you."

"The short chubby woman smiled and nodded. Now you are welcome, so go on your way, I know you have a way to go. Safe journey and God's blessing on you both."

Just then, a skinny dog bounded up to them and ran around their legs. "Come here you daft berserker," laughed Mrs. Hubbard, "Come on now and I'll fetch you a bone."

They waved and set off once more at a brisk pace. They held hands. A new sense of adventure raced through them and filled them with energy. It was a fair day, the breeze was warm and the sky clear. They passed farmed fields in various shades of green, and at one high point they could see for quite some distance across the vale.

"It's so beautiful," smiled Connie.

"When the sun shines," laughed Eddie. "I've seen some places that really take your breath away."

"They can't have been more beautiful than here."

"White sands, crystal-clear oceans and swaying palm trees... oh yes, my girl, they're more beautiful than 'ere."

"Tell me about some of the things you have seen."

Eddie regaled her with vivid tales and descriptions of the Caribbean Islands and of the home the pirates had created on Nassau. Though the small town was still there, the pirates were all long gone. With each tale he told, Connie's perception of the world grew and grew, until she realized how simple her life had been so far.

"When I was a lad in London, I knew a woman who had a habit of laying a heavy hand upon her husband. He put on a proud face, but we all pitied him the more. Your bruises are fading, but I can't help but ponder on the life you had with Joseph, I was just thinking on how I would probably 'ave done for him, if he hadn't gone over the cliff. The image brought the memory of London rushing in. Life is a weird and complex thing, isn't it? I don't understand the cruelty that some people inflict upon each other. Now to run a man down with a sword in a fair fight, that's quite a different thing... before you rush to put me down!"

Connie brought to her imagination the image of the woman battering her husband. "And he never left her?"

"On the day I left London, he still stood by his vows. I used to think to myself… soft-lad, and you'll never get me falling in love if that is the result."

"But he was just one man, surely? I should imagine it is normally the other way around."

"Aye, there's not many a woman who beats her husband, well to my knowledge, although we never know what goes on behind closed doors. Still, fists and pans are not the only weapons that women use. I believe their nagging tongues are what wear men down the most."

"Good Lord! Why on earth do you want to marry me, if your thoughts of women are so entirely negative?"

"I would tell you, but you've already scolded me for my flowery words so I think I'll keep them in my 'ead, thank you very much."

After a fair few steps in silence, Eddie asked, "Do you think you may grow to love me, even a little?"

"I don't think love is easily gained, neither by soft words nor in a short period of time. Ask me again in seven years; if you are still devotedly attached to my side, why maybe then I'll profess that true love exists betwixt us."

"Seven years? I'll give you another seven weeks. If you're not declaring love to me every day by then, well I'll eat my hat!"

Connie flicked her new shawl at him so it hit him in the arm, but she was laughing. "Oh, but good gracious, your fair face has addled your perception of reality!"

They were soon into Brixton, and their excitement about getting closer to Plymouth rose with every step. As they ambled along the main street, a few people passed them by. Raising their hats and wishing them a most prosperous day.

"I've never been blessed so many times before," marveled Connie as she happily replied with the same cheery greeting to all they met.

Eddie caused them to stop in front of an ancient perpendicular church. If asked, he wouldn't be able to explain, but he suddenly knew this is where he wanted to get married. So quintessentially English, so rural and pleasant, he could think of no better place.

He turned to Connie, "Well my girl, this is it. Let's find the vicar and get the deed done."

"Should I yoke myself to a scoundrel and throw all respectability to the wind? I think not! Circumstances might have put me in a place of indifference, but for myself I would choose the freedom of respectability, whether poor or rich matters not, only that I am accepted and find a position within society where I am valued." With that scathing rebuke, she folded her arms across her chest.

He could see the myriad of thoughts running through her eyes, and knew she was trying to work out why she was protesting.

Eddie had spent many days confused by Connie's mixed signals. He knew that for her to trust a man again would be hard, he did understand that. But he also knew life was short, and not so long ago they had both nearly lost theirs. He longed with a desperate desire to protect her, and to remove her from all harm. He wanted to wrap her in loving tenderness. His heart quickened whenever she drew near to him. His insides lurched whenever he saw her. For the very first time in his life he wanted to be wed.

If he was being honest, the thought thoroughly shocked him. He'd always dreamt of children, and yet somehow had erased the need to have a wife to do so. He longed to give Connie the security and respectability she craved, but he also wanted to tie her to his side and to allow no other man to go near her again. With such thoughts, his temperature did rise and the beat of his heart quickened. He saw behind her mask of indifference. He observed the thoughts that flashed behind her eyes and he longed to let the caged-bird out so that she could soar. He kissed her. Bold and unashamed that they were outside where any might see. He kissed her until he felt her succumb to his passions. "I love you, I love you," he avowed. "Please say yes, Connie, or I shall die."

"Oh, very well, I see the benefit of it, I do."

Chapter 19

ALL MANNER OF EMOTIONS ran through Connie as she considered the very unromantic proposal she had just received. She hadn't really wanted to get married the first time, and she had certainly never planned to marry for a second time. If she did this, she would be giving up her dreams of freedom. Yet what choice did she really have? Moreover, if she didn't go with Eddie to the New World, what was left for her?

"You bribed a man of God?"

"I did."

"Eddie that is thoroughly wicked, how could you do that?"

"Because I want to keep you safe, and I want to protect you every way I can, and by marrying me you'll be protected from the unwelcome advances of unscrupulous men. Besides, his church roof is leaking and he has assured me that one gold doubloon will definitely be enough to repair it as to make it almost brand new."

"You gave him a doubloon?"

"I did. Is my act of heresy not so offensive to you now?"

"It is not. At least some good will come from it."

Eddie grinned. "You're going to say *I do* then?"

"Well you make it sound like I have no choice!"

"No Connie, I won't have that. You'll never be able to say I forced you into this. If you really find the thought of spending your life with me so unbearable then for goodness' sake, say no!"

"You take offense like a woman!"

"And you insult like a man!"

They were almost face-to-face in their heated spat.

With timely (or Godly) intervention, the Vicar of St Mary's Chapel appeared as if from nowhere and announced, "If I may interject? I have found a witness, if you are willing, I will perform the ceremony now."

Connie and Eddie burst out laughing. Eddie offered an elbow, to which Connie hooked an arm, and then the two of them followed the short, bald vicar inside. The humble, cool, building that had stood for hundreds of years seemed to embrace them, and tranquility bounced between the stone walls. The ancient stained-glass, medieval roof bosses, ornate bench ends, and ornamental rood screen cast a timeless whisper of worship. The laughter that had bubbled so brightly a moment before, faded and left them sober and keenly alert to the seriousness of their undertaking.

"I will say the words," whispered Connie as they walked towards the front of the church, "but don't expect me to *actually* obey you!"

"My dear, I would be disappointed if you did!"

Looking up at the arched stained glass, Connie felt the impact of decades of worship. Oh Lord, forgive us, forgive me, she thought, and for the first time in years believed that God drew close to her.

The ceremony was compact! In an obvious attempt to complete the deed before anyone arrived and could bear witness to his transgression, the vicar so rushed through the ceremony, they felt breathless just listening to him. When he completed the church register, he wrote:

> *On this day of the June 9th 1727, one Edmond Paul Calstock of no fixed abode, was joined in legal matrimony to one Constance Wakeham of Bigbury, Devonshire.*
>
> *The banns having been called in Bigbury, Devonshire.*

It was a lie, which he hoped God would be lenient with him.

Thanks given, the pair left Brixton and set off with renewed eagerness for Turnchapel and the ferry that would take them to Plymouth docks.

"I cannot hide my curiosity any longer, pray tell, where did you buy the ring?"

"Well... *that* is a story."

Connie groaned, "Oh, please tell me you didn't bribe anyone else?"

"You'll be happy about this I'm sure, I purchased it back in Yealmpton from a woman who was haggling over the price of bread. I said to myself – this is a woman in need, so I did."

"Don't tell me you gave her a doubloon?"

"I did! Are you not well pleased with me, wife!"

Connie snorted, "Husband, if the woman was well-attached to this ring, then I will make us about turn and go and give it back to her."

"She assured me her husband had long been in the ground, and *that* the very reason for her poor position. I swear to you, she could not give me the ring fast enough!"

"I think I've married a Robin Hood of the seas."

"Art thou my fair Marion, then? If so, you may call me by any name you choose."

Connie giggled, and it was a delight to his ears.

"You know wife, you have taught me to be friendly, an art that is neither easy nor common. I thought my days of piracy would surely be my days until my demise, and yet here I am... no longer longing for the swordplay of battle and the deviousness of sneaking upon an ill-equipped ship. You have indeed created in me a new man."

"Where did you learn to speak with such flourishes? Bless my socks but it irritates my ears so. Why can you not simply say... Connie, I'm no longer a pirate." The last part said in mocking deep voice.

"I don't talk like that."

She raised an eyebrow, "Umm-hmm."

Along the way, they accepted the inquisitive glances of passersby with a smile and a question, to check they were still on the right pathways. Excitement was building inside Connie, she might be attached to a man again, and a wife once more, but she had such an adventure stretched out before her that she almost whooped aloud for joy. However, not wanting Eddie to believe her excitement stemmed from the fact that he strode beside her, she remained quiet. When she reflected on it, she caught her breath at the craziness of having been single such a short time. All her dreams! Those daydreams of a life on her own, gone, puff, just like that, and all because she had gazed upon a pair of beautiful blue eyes and lost her head!

The hill down into Turnchapel dock was immensely steep, and when a horse and cart approached them on the way up the hill, she was totally amazed they could make it. Down they rushed into the one street village, busy now in the early evening with fishermen pulling in their boats and mooring up for the night.

"Does the ferry still run?" asked Eddie.

"Old Fred'll be doin' one last crossing, you'll find him at the end of the pier," answered a well-weathered old man, with a clay pipe dangling from his lips, which he didn't remove even when he spoke.

They rushed along the rickety wooden pier. Eddie called out to a man who was untying his ropes. "Are you Fred, sir? And if so we would like passage across the Sound if you will."

The sailor took off his cap and waved it at them as answer. "It's tuppence a ride," he said preparing to leave.

"Sir, we have no coin on us right now, but take us across and tomorrow I'll meet you on the Barbican when you come in and give two shillings instead."

"Do you know how many a time I've heard that? Go on away with ya. Ya can walk all around the River Plym for all I care, and take you three days to do it. I wasn't born yesterday!"

Connie leaned close and whispered to Eddie, "What a curse having nothing but gold doubloons is!" But she was laughing. "Sir," said Connie taking a step closer and taking off her wedding ring. "I offer you this in good faith. It is worth something, is it not? You may hold on to it until my husband here (and now it was hard not to giggle) brings you the two shillings tomorrow."

He took the ring, examined it, and then put it in his pocket. "Very well," he said, "go on down."

Going down the rope ladder and into the boat, turned out to be quite a task for Connie in her shoes that didn't really fit her well, and her long skirts. Without Eddie's steadying hand, she was sure she would have tipped right into the sea.

The ferryman rowed them across the water. As they approached Plymouth, Eddie asked, "Do you know where we might find clean rooms?" He'd stayed in Plymouth before, and had left his residence covered in flea bites. Whereas he could take a little torture, he didn't want to submit Connie to such a thing.

"The Minerva is here on the Barbican, if it's not full, they offer clean rooms and tasty food. My second-cousin Jonathan is the proprietor; you can tell 'im old Fred sent you. Not sure it'll do you any good like, but you can tell 'im nevertheless." His smoking long-pipe wagged up and down as he spoke.

"Hey up," he called to a young lad waiting for him along the Barbican dock. He threw the rope line to the lad who deftly tied it to a mooring bollard. "Here, Jim, take these two 'ere along to Jonathan's will ya, there's a good lad."

Jim didn't have far to take them, for they had moored a very short distance from the Minerva Inn. Outside the inn, Eddie turned to Jim. "Listen lad, I've no coin on me at the moment, but I've a need for a helping hand over the next two days, if your hands could be them, well I'll pay you grandly before we leave."

"See that bollard over there," said Jim.

"Aye," said Eddie.

"Well, most of the day I'm sat right there waiting for boats to come in. So just come and fetch me when you've a need."

"I will indeed," replied Eddie.

Not too far from where they were standing was a wooden building used to sell fish. Although it was closed for the day now, the stench of fish was overpowering and Connie couldn't help scrunching her nose. The Minerva Inn looked like a respectable place. The whitewash was bright and clean, and the black wood of the lower part of the building gleamed in a well-kept manner.

"I'm sure there will be a more pleasant smell inside," grinned Eddie. He ducked low and entered, and Connie followed. Indeed, inside the smell that tickled their noses was that of ale and tobacco.

The place was fairly packed, and when no innkeeper came to greet them, Eddie forged his way towards the bar. It wasn't long before a tall, beanpole of a man spotted them and approached them on the other side of the bar. He didn't appear to be very old, and yet his face was lined and full of shadows. He raised one eyebrow and looked Connie up and down. "We're a respectable place," he muttered.

"Good sir, this is my wife. You will excuse our shabby appearance, but we were held up by bandits on our journey to Plymouth (not a lie), and lost our entire luggage to them, (rather a big lie). Do you have rooms for us? We might stay a few days for we sail to the Americas thereafter."

"You with the religious lot then?" the innkeeper asked.

Eddie wasn't sure which would gain them quicker residency, in the end he decided to be honest. "No sir, we're not. But we travel to the same place."

Jonathan visibly relaxed. "Can't stand them religious lot," he laughed. "Don't drink do 'ay, no good for coffers and that's for sure.

Eddie laughed along to be polite.

"Well come on, let me take you straight to your room," he picked up the bar hatch and came to their side of it. "But wait, if you've been robbed like, how are you going pay?"

"If you'll give me until tomorrow morning, I'll pay you in advance of our room and food, if it please you?"

"Yep, please me right enough, but if you fancy spending a night and then making a dash for it, I'd best warn you that the Minerva has a reputation about her for not being too pleasant, and I wouldn't want your pretty missus here to feel the blunt of it… if you get my gist!"

"Sir, I get your gist full well. Have no fear, we're honest folk and I'll pay you in full on the morrow."

"Well in that case, come along now, for today is busy and my time precious enough."

Seeing as they hadn't bargained a price for their room, Jonathan saw an opportunity to rent out his most expensive bed, he'd add a shilling or two on the top of it, of course, for having to wait for payment.

He led them up a spiral staircase and along to a room that sat directly over the lounge. "Shall I send up a bite for supper?" he asked as he opened the door.

"That would be splendid, anything will do that is quick for it has been a long time since breakfast."

The door closed behind them as they came in and Jonathan went hurrying downstairs.

"Oh Eddie, the room is wonderful!" said Connie.

The whitewashed walls were interjected with heavy black wooden beams. A wooden bed sat to one side and on the other a table and two chairs. The paned-window looked out over the harbor.

A fire had been set but not lit, and Eddie bent straight away to lift a flint box left ready. "Shall I light the fire? It is not so cold in here."

"Please light it, I will appreciate a good wash, and the warmth will be nice."

Eddie set to lighting the fire. When he stood up again, there was a moment of awkwardness between them. Eddie gulped and didn't understand why he was suddenly so nervous, as they had spent the previous few nights together.

As if reading his thoughts, Connie said, "Maybe it is because we're now married?"

"Maybe."

"Tell me what you have in mind for tomorrow."

"That depends on what I can find out this evening."

"You're going out?"

"I need to see the captains of the ships moored in dock and see if any of them are going to America and whether they have space for us. I'll be as quick as a flash."

He gave her a quick hug. "When the food comes don't wait for me, I'll eat when I return."

Not long after he'd gone there was a knock on the bedroom door. On opening the door, a maid entered carrying a large tray with its contents covered by a cloth. "Johnny said you wanted something quick, so I've fetched you up a cold spread, is that alright?"

"That's perfect, thank you," answered Connie.

Although Eddie had told her to eat without him, Connie found she couldn't. She took off her shoes and lay down on the bed to wait for him.

"Wake up beautiful," coaxed Eddie two hours later.

Connie sat up immediately, rubbing her eyes. "How did it go?"

"We're going to *Pennsylvania!*"

Connie jumped off the bed. "We are!"

"We are!"

They laughed and jumped about holding hands.

"Now that we have passage on a ship to America, it's vital that I find a businessman willing to exchange our coins."

"Do we have any left?" laughed Connie.

Eddie grinned, "Aye, one or two!"

"You're not going to look now are you?"

"No, but I must rise very early and set about it. Now, what do we have here?" He pulled back the cloth covering the tray; both eager to see what lay beneath. A feast was before their eyes, slices of ham, cheese, bread, pickles and a flagon of ale. They sat at the table and dived in, too hungry to talk as they spread butter on their bread and covered it with thick slices of meat and cheese.

When she'd finished, Connie sat back with a sigh. "That was so good!"

"You still look tired," said Eddie.

Indeed, Connie's eyes had begun to feel heavy as soon as she'd finished eating. "We've walked a good distance, and our sleep last night wouldn't keep anyone going."

"Then let's retire."

They took it in turns to wash in the cold water left in the jug in the washbowl and then slipped beneath the covers. Eddie automatically put out his arm, and Connie moved to lay her head on his firm chest. Surprisingly, neither of them went to sleep, in fact both suddenly seemed to have found a renewed energy.

"Will you talk to me? I think it will help me to relax."

Eddie kissed her forehead. "These last few days I've been putting much thought to my past. I never planned to be a pirate you know, it's important you understand that. When I was five and ten, the appeal of the sea seemed romantic and adventurous. I couldn't wait for my travels to begin."

His wistful tone told Connie a sailor's life had not turned out to be as his young mind had dreamt. "I grew, not only in height, but in understanding that the world is not fair. My heart hardened with each passing year, with the thought that my freedom could only be bought with wealth and nothing else. I cared less if I would ever be happy, but I would be damned rather than be poor! It drove me until I became a man I didn't recognize. Dead men hang around my neck like millstones. One day I fear they'll have me sink beyond despair and regret into the pits of hell."

"Don't talk like that. Would you leave me and set me adrift in a world I know nothing about? How would I survive?"

"You're a mighty strong lass, Connie, you would survive I'm sure."

Right then she wasn't sure she wanted to be on her own. "It's been years since I went to church and even when I went it was to be an obedient daughter to my parents. But certain words have remained with me, a verse here and there. The truth of them I cannot confirm, but Jesus takes our sins away is what I'm sure the Good Book says."

"One of the crew of the Rosalie, was a woman called Long-cup Cathy."

"One of the pirates was a woman?"

Eddie nodded.

She didn't know why, but somehow knowing that one of the pirates that died on that beach was a woman caused an upset inside her.

"Cathy and I had a great friendship."

A little jealousy stirred in Connie, and she wondered what he was about to share.

"Cathy was long in the tooth when I joined the crew; it was she who taught me nearly everything I needed to know about sailing ships... and piracy. Yet, it's her reflective thoughts that linger with me most. One day I was so frustrated that I couldn't leave the Rosalie, that I wanted to run Hawkins through. She took me aside, gave me a rum and then told me something I will never forget. 'Earnest,' she said to me, 'anger burns goodness right out of your heart, leaving behind a dried shriveled organ that can barely function. The life source of a hater becomes brittle and hard to bear. Forgiveness is like healing honey and oils the substance of the soul, giving it back its life and flexibility and delivering peace.' The trouble is I can't ask those I've killed to forgive me, so I'm caught neither able to give or receive forgiveness. I think it'll make my days short."

These humble acknowledgments stirred Connie's heart more than any of his ardent flowery demonstrative words ever could. She sat up and took his face in her hands. "So long as the spirit is willing a man may change his ways and take a step into tomorrow with new resolve and hope." Her lips came softly upon his, touching with the lightness of a feather. He moaned, his body instantly stirring to life.

"My girl," he whispered huskily. His hands pressed around her back and pulled her down on top of him. "Connie." He kissed her cheeks and trailed his lips down to nibble her earlobe. She moaned and pressed her hips tight against his body. He needed no other encouragement. He swung her round in one swift move and maneuvered so that he was now on top of her. They clung to each other with a new desperate need. A passion burned between them. As he came into her and claimed her as his wife, she surrendered to the waves of tingles that washed over her. She was the fisherman's wife no longer. All the torment of her past slipped from her bones and left her light-headed and giddy. She was now a pirate's wife, Mrs. Edmond Calstock, and happiness surged through her every pore.

Chapter 20

EDDIE HAD LEFT THE ROOM quite some time before Connie stirred. Knowing she had overslept and there was much to accomplish, she'd sprung out of bed, dressed and gone in search of someone who could help her.

In the kitchen she found both the cook and her niece to be full of ideas about where she could make her purchases. Wasting no time she set off to explore and to place orders for wares that she would collect either later that day (when Eddie hopefully returned with small change) or the following morning before they set sail. However, on stepping outside the door she saw Eddie rushing forward with a grin and a wave. Jim rushed behind him with a travel trunk on a cart.

"For all our shopping!" declared Eddie when they arrived at her side. "Go on in, Jim, and fetch it to our room – the bar keep or one of the girls will show you the way."

"Right-ee-ho Earnest Ed," laughed Jim.

"Earnest?" said Connie.

Eddie laughed, I told him I was a pirate but confessed to only be spinning him a yarn, 'twas but an amusement."

"Umm," murmured Connie not convinced.

"I found a man who deals with money, who has exchanged our doubloons for more commonly used coin. Shillings and pounds will ensure we become less visible."

"And he didn't ask where the gold came from?"

"I first met with a most obliging tailor who dropped everything when he heard how much I'd pay, and with his good assistant set about adapting an outfit, ordered by another, to fit me. He assured me it's the latest fashion. Do you approve?"

He gave her a little bow and stood back so she could admire his attire.

"Dark blue suits you very well." She didn't bother to mention that it highlighted even more the light and sparkle of his blue eyes which were now somehow even more bewitching than before. "Although, I am sure whoever the suit was made for will not be well pleased when he finds it is no longer ready!"

"The tailor insisted that the purchaser of the outfit is not due into Plymouth for another week, and therefore he has plenty of time to make another, so all's well."

Eddie led her back inside. "Let's partake of food before we embark on the rest of the day and 'ere – I have something for you." He handed her the wedding ring.

"Thank you," she smiled and slipped it onto her ring finger.

As Eddie watched her lack of enthusiasm for the ring a flicker of guilt touched him. "You know when we're settled I'll buy a far prettier ring for you. This simple posy ring is only temporary."

Her smile was soft. "The ring is perfectly fine and does not need to be changed. I was just remembering how Joseph had given me his mother's posy ring when we married, but when he was short of money he took it back and sold it."

He was too choked up to tell her he had every intention of buying her something that would be special to them, and it would most definitely be engraved with their names, that he determined to do.

He led them into the empty lounge and went in search of the innkeeper. Connie took a moment to look around the inn. The black timber beams and dark wood furniture did little to liven up the room, and even though the sun was high in the sky, hardly any light entered through the small paned windows. She was glad when the kitchen maid appeared with a lamp that she hung from a hook over their table. "Didn't get far then, miss," smiled the girl in a friendly manner.

"Indeed not," answered Connie.

Eddie, having ordered, then went upstairs to check the chest and put away the money. He also had a little gift for his new wife he wanted to attend to. When he came back, he sat on the edge of his seat and placed an elbow on the table. "Where was I? Oh, I know, dressed to impress! I'd hoped the merchant would perceive I was a man of means, however, there was something about his somewhat eagle-eye and raised brow that encouraged me to believe he saw straight through my ruse. The blaggard, for that is what he was, took a very high interest but I was in no position to haggle too hard, for I could tell by his constant appraising me up and down and by the glint in his eye that he knew me for my true self! How then could I blame him for demanding such a high cut?"

Connie placed a hand on his arm. "The most important thing, surely, is that we are rid of it? I for one would not fancy going into haberdashery for example, and requesting to buy my buttons or ribbons with a gold doubloon!"

"So, you're to go shopping?"

"I'll need more than the clothes I wear, Eddie Calstock!"

He laughed, but it was a soft and happy sound and not at all a teasing one. "I too plan to visit traders today. What say you to going our separate ways? Will you be staunch enough to broker you own purchases?"

"I will indeed, and I'm sure I'll find some amusement in it as well for I have never in my life been into a place where I can buy material and have it made into a dress for me overnight!"

"They do that here?"

"Yes, the cook informed me of a place of good repute. Where will you go?"

"I'm for the hardware stores. I have been informed that the price of equipment in the Americas is three-fold what it is 'ere, so I'll stock us with as much as I think we'll need and be able to manage in the transportation for wherever we are sent upon our arrival. We'll need rakes and shovels, twine and all manner of things for your farm, sweet Connie."

"Our farm."

They leaned forward until their foreheads we're touching. "Our farm," he repeated, before lowering his lips to hers.

The kitchen maid appeared again just then, and they drew apart but their eyes lingered on each other. They thought they would be too excited to partake of a large meal, but when the plates turned up with eggs and bacon on top of fresh baked bread they dived in and didn't surface again until their plates were clear. Eddie laughed when Connie used a small piece of bread to mop the grease from her plate.

"I've put the bulk of our money in a secret compartment in the chest, I'll show you how to find it later," said Eddie. "Take this for now, but if you need more you should take it without asking, for it is half yours." He handed her a lady's purse.

Connie's mouth opened. She had never owned such a thing in her life. A small knitted bag with a silk lining and a little drawstring handle so she could tie it to her wrist. Inside were a number of notes that stunned her.

"Thank you," she said and her eyes filled with tears.

"You're welcome." He didn't say anything, but the sight of her appreciation greatly moved him.

"I won't need all this money," she said quietly, while tying the purse to her wrist.

"Spend what you will, it's yours. Shall we go? I'll walk with you part of the way into town. Jim's waiting outside, apparently the stores I need are far apart and I'll need him to lead the way to save time."

"Yes, let's go."

Jim jumped up from the floor where he'd been sitting as soon as he saw them. He'd already taken payment to the ferryman and accepted a good amount for himself. He was more than happy to donate all his time to this man who didn't seem to understand the true value of money.

The bustle of Plymouth was something startlingly new to Connie. She'd never seen so many people in her life. The most she'd ever seen together was on Mothering Sunday, when all the local churches walked many miles to join the main church in the parish in one tremendous service of thanksgiving. She could fit those two hundred souls a hundred times over, in the docks and streets around her.

Eddie held her hand tight and pulled her along behind him as he and Jim pushed their way through the crowds. They headed away from the fish markets and the wharf where several barque ships were moored. She was glad to leave the overwhelming stench of fish behind them. Well used to the sea and all it offered, this was however, more pungent and offensive and she could only assume a measure of dead fish lay splattered across the cobbles of the quay.

It didn't take long to leave the Barbican behind them and reach the busy streets of commerce. For a little while they almost forgot about their mission to purchase the things they needed. Both of them were in awe of the different shops and the number of people walking the cobbled streets. Suddenly, a wonderful smell wafted around them.

"What's that?" Connie asked Jim.

"That's pasties," answered Jim.

"They smell wonderful," said Eddie.

"If you've not had one before, you really should buy some. Inside the pastry are beef, potato, and turnip. They keep you goin' all day they do."

"Oh, we have to buy some Eddie, we can try them later."

They approached the woman with a tray full of pasties hanging on a rope that went around her neck. "How much?" Eddie asked.

"Why, one and four to such a looker as yer'self me lover," the woman replied with a wink.

Eddie took out his purse and paid her for two, then passed the pasties that were wrapped in paper to Connie.

"Thank you, kindly," said Eddie, tipping a hand to his hat.

The woman laughed, "Oh, yer welcome, me lover." Then she went on her way crying out words that were too hard for Connie to understand. Eddie turned to look at Connie.

"Will you be alright from 'ere on? I'll meet you back at the Minerva when we're done."

"Yes, of course," smiled Connie. And then Eddie did the most natural thing, he leaned in and kissed her on the cheek, in a way that any old-married couple might do. The gesture both warmed and embarrassed her.

They had left her outside the haberdashery store that the cook had mentioned, hesitantly Connie entered. A bell above the door jingled as she went in. The large store was already quite busy, and Connie began to move around, feasting her eyes on the rolls of cloth and the counters laden with reels of ribbon and button boxes. There was so much choice she didn't know where to begin. Connie's eyes were not only on the goods, but traveled around the room taking in the sight of the people all around. The women in the room were bonneted and shawled in striking colors she'd never seen in material before. Bluebell dresses, primrose shawls, purple-heather ribbons to name but a few. The view was striking and caused the realization that she had been stowed away indeed, in a very tiny hole in this huge world they lived in, one filled with grays and browns and even those lacked luster. A sudden and unexpected excitement stirred within her. Maybe she was an adventurer after all? But whether she was or was not, one thing she knew… These well-to-do folk, in their finery were another breed to her entirely. She did not feel comfortable in their presence, even though they seemed kindly, and the ladies had exchanged a smile with her as they wandered around. She was a worker, she understood this well. The toil of the land, the pulling of nets, the cooking and cleaning were all a part of her and though the fortune Eddie had stashed in their chest could offer her a life such as these fine peacocks, she did not want it.

She almost fled out of the shop, but a woman with a kindly face approached. "How can I serve you today?"

Connie hesitated, feeling totally out of her depth. The woman at once understood. "Do you know… we had some blue cloth arrive just last week from France, it is the perfect color to match your eyes, could I show it to you?"

Connie nodded and a good deal of her stress slipped away as she found herself in kindly and capable hands.

"I was told that you also make dresses here, and that if I pay extra they can be made ready for tomorrow morning?" She looked at the shop assistant for confirmation, for in truth she found that quite impossible to believe.

The woman smiled. "That is true. We have several women who will sew through the night to ensure an order is fulfilled."

"That must be a strain on their eyes," Connie blurted out without thinking.

"We have the room lighter than day with all our lamps, they can see just fine."

Connie squirmed as she received the gentle rebuke.

"Now this is the cloth I referred to. What kind of dress did you have in mind?"

"I need two dresses if that is possible?"

"It is. Are they for anything in particular, do you need an evening gown?"

"Oh goodness no!" The shop assistant raised her eyebrows at Connie's tone. "I mean... I have no need for an evening gown. We're sailing for the Americas tomorrow and I'll require two day dresses if you please."

"You're going to the New World?" asked a young serving girl who had overheard and was instantly by Connie's side.

"Yes indeed, my husband secured us passage yesterday."

"I've heard it is a terrible place, full of savages, I would be afraid to go," said the young girl.

"Mary!" snapped the woman serving Connie.

"It's fine," Connie assured the older woman, then turning back to the young girl she said, "Eddie has been before. He says it's a wonderful place and a land of opportunity."

By now four of the shop assistants had gathered around her. Suddenly, they were all firing questions at her. She tried her best to answer, but for the most part she didn't know the answer herself. When they discovered that she had only married such a short while ago, their manner quickly changed from curiosity to a need to supply her every need.

"I now understand the reason for the distress of your dress," said the older assistant. "Held at gunpoint by highwaymen, how awful. And you with nothing to wear but this dress ever since, oh dear, you poor, poor thing. Chop-chop girls back to work, we have much to do and not much time."

Lots of different rolls of cloth were held up for her to choose from until she felt her head begin to spin. When the assistant realized they were swamping Connie, she shooed away all but two young girls.

"You are a good-looking woman, tall for a woman but very bonny. You have a take-no-nonsense stride when you walk, which is perhaps not so attractive. But you look a picture of health and strong, I can understand why your husband snapped you up after such a short acquaintance. Most marriages are for convenience, a wife then is for helping her husband in his affairs and to bear his children so his line can carry on. Love is not required, although often it grows. You are lucky indeed, to have found a man to marry who you so clearly love. You are the envy of every young girl here today, and that is the truth. Bad luck… well bad men, might have robbed you of your trousseau but we will soon amend that, we have absolutely everything you need here!"

"Except hats," said one of the young girls.

"Except shoes and boots," said the other.

Connie laughed.

Later, and much exhausted, Connie and Eddie returned to their room in the Minerva.

Eddie pulled the chair away from the table for Connie to sit. Connie stared at it with a weird expression on her face.

"What is it?" asked Eddie.

She shook her head. "No one has ever pulled out a chair for me before, it caused me to experience an odd sensation that I can't quite put into words."

When she was seated, Eddie crouched by her side and put his hand on her arm. "When we reach the New World, I will ensure you're treated like a lady always. You shall live your life in comfort Connie Calstock, of that I promise you. Whatever you desire, I shall do my best to obtain it."

Connie waited until he had sat down opposite her. She gazed at the man in whom she had put all her trust. "I want land, Eddie. I want to build and produce. I want a place where I can grow trees from the pips I carry in my pockets. Could we be farmers? Would you be able to settle if that was all your lot in life contained?"

"Yes and a thousand times yes! And now let's eat these pasties for I'm famished!"

Chapter 21

ON THE LONDON TO PLYMOUTH ROAD a stagecoach raced. Its driver gently flicked the whip against the side of his main runner to keep up their fast pace. Inside the coach sat three passengers, picked up at the Yealmpton Inn stop. The previous passengers all cast out at the point of three pistols. On promise of his life and a large payment the driver raced, with speed he'd never done before, towards the port of Plymouth. He tried to avoid potholes and ruts but at this particular part of the road it was hard to do. His cape flew behind him and sweat dripped from his brow.

Inside the coach three men were unceremoniously tossed from side-to-side, and many curses flew from their mouths. Nevertheless, they didn't call for the driver to slow, for they needed speed. In fact, time was of the essence. There was a ship preparing to sail and by hook or by crook they would reach the port before it left.

Chapter 22

TODAY THEY WOULD BOARD the *Adventurer*, and when the tide was high, they'd set sail for the Americas and a brand new life. Connie woke filled to overflowing with excitement. Never had she imagined back in Bigbury-on-Sea, that the world was so large. She could hardly contain the buzz of adventure she felt.

There was still much to do, and they dressed and packed their purchases into the new travel chest with haste. Taking a handle each, they carried the chest with much laughter as they bumped into walls and doors and eventually arrived in the lounge.

"We'll collect this shortly, pray keep it safe until we return," Eddie told the innkeeper.

"I will watch over it," the man answered. "Your breakfast is waiting on the table for you, just go through. Dolly will serve you some fresh coffee to wash it down."

They watched the docks come to life through the window as they hurried through a spread of cold meats, various cheeses, and bread. The coffee was too bitter for Connie and she asked for a cider instead.

"We sail in six hours. Will you amuse yourself when I go to make sure our supplies are all loaded on board?"

"I'm going back to the dressmakers, she promised to have my dresses ready by this morning. So yes, I'll be fine. Will you collect me here? I do not think I have courage enough to meet you on the ship. Have you seen the plank? The thought of walking across it when it sways so much has quite filled me with terror!"

Eddie laughed, and then leaned over the table to talk more quietly. "If you can survive a haunting my girl, the plank will be as nothing to you."

He left after that, eager to ensure all their crates were safely taken on board.

Connie finished her cider and then left for the busy streets of Plymouth. After two days of exploring, she was now confident on the streets to follow. She wove in and out of the growing crowd and made her way straight to the haberdashers on Main Street. A big brass bell tinkled when she opened the door and swept inside.

"Why here she is!" cried Mrs. Tucker. "Come girls, quick let us fit her out." They rushed Connie through to the back to their sewing room with giggles and excited chatter. Connie allowed herself to be swept along with their merry enthusiasm. They stripped off her clothes. "What shall I do with these?" asked Mrs. Tucker, holding Connie's old clothes.

"Can you wrap them for me please?" she asked.

Stripped of even her undergarments, Connie grew conscious and hurried them to dress her in her new bloomers. After that, they pulled on an attractive floral skirt, that reminded her of the meadow she'd sank into Eddie's arms, and then a corset was laced with stays and pulled tight until she could hardly breathe. "Steady on," she moaned. Her corset was a very pale pink and she loved it.

"You look right beautiful!" said Mrs. Tucker.

Connie felt pretty for the first time in her life. The cloth was soft and flowed with ease. She spun around with her arms wide, making her skirt swish.

"And you have the other one for me too?" she asked when she stopped spinning.

Mrs. Tucker smiled. "It is ready and wrapped."

"Thank you."

Payment exchanged and well wishes given. Holding a plethora of parcels Connie strutted like a new woman and proudly strode to the milliners to buy a bonnet.

So happy did she feel, and so brisk her step, that she failed to discern the shadow of a man that followed her.

Connie laughed gaily. "No, good sir, and thank you kindly, but a hat with peacock feathers is not for me! A simple straw bonnet is all I require." The tall thin man could not mask his displeasure, and beckoned a young man to come and serve her. Obviously, she was beneath his custom.

Hat purchased and secured under her chin by a pink ribbon to match her corset, Connie went with quick pace to another store that had caught her eye and imagination. 'William's Stationers' declared the sign that hung from fancy hooks on the wall over the door. She stepped inside and immediately breathed in the deep and wonderful aroma of ink and paper.

"Good day, madam. And how may I help you this fine morning?"

"I would very much like a book to record my daily activities, and I will of course need quill and ink, and… if you have such a thing, I will need some sort of case to carry them all in."

"You have come to the right place, the book you request is a diary, and we have plenty of bound books specifically for that purpose, please come this way."

Shortly after, Connie stepped back onto the street carrying yet another parcel. Her thoughts made her smile – I should hurry back before Eddie discovers I am a person of trivial matters after all! Again, she failed to notice that a man slipped from an alleyway as she left the shop, and kept a close distance behind her as she made her way back to the Minerva.

After placing her new purchases within their chest and re-locking it, she began to pace back and forth in the lounge. Now her shopping was complete, she could hardly contain her impatience to be on the way to the ship.

"Oh at last!" she cried when through the window she spotted Eddie fast approaching the inn. She hastened to the door, but before she could get there someone grabbed her arm. She spun to defend herself, automatically expecting a beating. A knife was thrust none too gently against her waist an inch below her corset so she could accurately ascertain its sharpness and the depth of trouble she was in.

"Do not scream, or it will be the last sound you make!" hissed a man in her ear.

She knew that voice! Dismay came, and her knees grew weak.

"This way." The man pushed her towards a table in the far corner by the door that led to the hallways and kitchens. "Sit."

She did as she was bid, but now her hands were shaking and her heart a flutter. Her mind though was battling anger. They had been so close to a new life, was it to be ripped away from them at the eleventh hour.

Snake-Eye leered at her and wrapped an arm around her shoulder. "Don't think I came on my own now do you?"

Eddie entered the inn and searched for her, when his eyes fell on the man with his arms wrapped around Connie his blood boiled. Before he had taken three steps across the room towards them, two men appeared, one at each of his sides.

"Steady matey, go slow. Don't make a fuss. Snake-Eye has a dagger to your lass's waist. One wrong move from you and she's a gonner, do you savvy?"

Eddie slowed his pace and nodded.

"What do you want Smiley?" he asked as they approached Connie's table.

"Just a friendly chat, my boy, mate-to-mate, that's all. Come and have yourself a seat now. Spike, fetch us some grog and plenty of it."

"Aye-aye Cap'n Smiley."

"Less of that you fool!"

"Sorry, Cap'n, but no one close, no harm done." Smiley scowled at him, and Spike rushed away to the bar.

"No, no, my boy," said Smiley when Eddie went to sit next to Connie. "You sit here right next to me, *see…*" he indicated to his hand, and when Eddie looked, he beheld a pistol pointing in his direction.

"You can't kill us you'd never get out of Plymouth alive; everyone here will bear witness to it."

"I never said I was going to kill you now did I. Calm yourself down boy and no one will get hurt." When Eddie had sat down on the edge of his seat, Smiley sat down too.

"Do you know," said Smiley, "that the Minerva was used by press-gangs? There's peepholes about the walls from behind which the press-gangs would look for potential sailors entering the establishment. If a fellow appeared strong and healthy, when he wasn't looking they'd slip a King's shilling in his beer, if the unsuspecting patron drank the beer then the press-gang would jump out and state the poor fellow had accepted the King's coin and then they'd cart 'im off to join the Navy. There are secret passageways behind these 'ere walls. And do you know how I know that? Well, let me tell you, I've been here before. That door," he said nodding to the door that led to the kitchens. "That door is just a hop and a skip from our departure. No one will see where we go and so if we do kill you… and I'm not saying we are going to kill you, but if we do, well then… our escape is well planned."

"What do you want?"

"Why the map of course."

"What map?" asked Eddie.

Smiley looked at Snake-Eye, and he in turn pressed the knife more harshly into Connie's skin. She yelped.

"Hush your mouth woman, for it's not only you who will end up on the floor as dead as dead can be."

Connie gulped and tried to stop her trembling.

The Burr Island pirates were almost unrecognizable. Gone were their obvious pirate garb and accessories, in their place common sailor attire clothed them. If it wasn't for their scars they might have blended in without any scrutiny.

"So, I'll ask you again, and you had better pipe up the truth, because I don't think the next jibe from Snake-Eye will be a threat."

To enforce Smiley's words, Snake-Eye pushed the dagger even more. Connie jumped but managed to remain silent as she swallowed her gulp of pain and fright.

Spike returned with a tray of small glasses and a bottle of rum and placed it on the table.

"Let's drink to your good health," laughed Smiley. Everyone knocked back a small tumbler of rum, even Connie.

"How did you find us?" Eddie asked.

Smiley put an elbow on the table and leaned forward. "When you leave a trail of crumbs the way you did, it was easy. Gold doubloons' boy, well they're not often seen by common folk now are they? So when they appear they do set tongues a-wagging." He laughed, 'ha-ha-ha' and Spike and Snake-Eye joined in. "And there I was thinking Earnest Eddie had brains in his head, seems he don't have any after all."

Connie couldn't help snorting down her nose. Eddie knew that if they ever got out of this alive, she would rub his ears sore with her told-you-so's. Smiley looked between them and then 'ha-ha-ha' roared from his chest again.

"Well I'll be darned if you didn't go and fall in love eh, you stupid pirate! Don't you know women are nothing but bad luck for us?"

"He's not a pirate any longer!" hissed Connie.

"You'd best batten down your hatches till you're spoken to, wench!" snarled Smiley, all laughter now gone.

She quickly snapped her mouth closed; she knew what antagonizing this man could bring.

Smiley poured himself another rum and knocked it back in one. "Now, about the map…"

Eddie looked at Connie and knew he had no choice, she had stolen his heart. Nothing else in the world mattered now – not even treasure. "It seems I'm caught between the Devil and the Deep Blue Sea. Tell Snake-Eye to back off. I 'ave it in my pocket."

"Then let's be having it," snarled Smiley.

"First, give me your word on the Pirate's Oath that you'll let us go."

"I swear," Smiley spat on his palm and offered his hand to Eddie.

Eddie shook it, then reached inside his jacket pocket and pulled out a folded piece of paper.

"You have a treasure map?" asked Connie askance.

Eddie gave her a little shrug. "I was going to tell you about it once we'd set sail."

"And I could no longer leave you!"

"I didn't plan for us to go after it, so I thought it didn't matter."

"Then why do you still have it?"

"Now, now, me lovers, as touching as it is to watch a lovers' tiff, none of us have time for it. Pass it over."

With a face full of reluctance, Eddie handed over the map. Smiley unfolded the paper and laid it out on the table. It was small and the writing tiny, but quick as a flash Smiley declared, "This here is the Caribbean."

"It is," answered Eddie.

"And this cross, this marks the spot where you and Hawkins hid the treasure?"

"It is."

Smiley folded the paper back up with haste, and pushed it inside one of his pockets. He nodded towards Snake-Eye, who removed both his arm from Connie's shoulder and the dagger from her side.

"Tell me matey… is it true that within this here hoard sits the Delilah Diamond?"

Eddie didn't answer.

Connie couldn't hide her interest. "What's the Delilah Diamond?" she asked addressing Eddie.

Eddie licked his lips, his whole mouth felt as dry as sawdust. "'Tis nothing but a rumor," he answered, "no truth to it."

"The legend of the Delilah Diamond is that she is *reputedly* the purest and largest blue diamond ever found," said Smiley his eyes glistening with excitement. "Alexander the Great was said to have found her in India and stole her from King Porus. Because of the bloodshed of the Indians, they cursed the stone and legends of disasters follow whoever finds her. So the Delilah is as famous for the downfall of every man who handles her as she is for her size."

"Well then, you 'ave your answer – for I'm still 'ere and therefore my hand can never have touched her!" Eddie offered his hands forward, as if the absence of the stone now would reflect the fact that he'd never had it.

"But Hawkins has gone now hasn't he, and maybe it was him that handled the precious stone while you watched on."

"Captain Smiley, you have a reputation which I greatly respect. It's said you're the finest sailor that ever sailed the seas, and no one knows the currents like you do. I wanted to be like you, respected by my crew and feared by all others who sail the oceans. But nearly drowning changed me, that and Connie here, for I never thought to love a woman as I do her. So I tell you the truth when I say… the Delilah is not part of the treasure that you seek, there is wealth there, but not the diamond that so many search for."

Smiley regarded Eddie for a long minute; silence cocooned them, though in the distance people's chatter continued, pipes were smoked and staff rushed around the tavern to serve.

"We're going now, and we're going to let you go to find your new life, for I'm a man of my word. However…" and now the old pirate leaned forward, and placed his pistol on the wooden table. "If… it turns out that there is no treasure at this cross you've given me, well then you best pray I don't find you.

Because I will come for you, and when you least expect it, I'll appear and soon have your bodies feeding the fishes. Is that understood Earnest Eddie?"

"Very clearly," answered Eddie, who sneaked a hand under the table to hold Connie's hand.

"Arr, love-birds ain't you? Well listen up my cockatoos, I've already set foot in Philadelphia and have friends thereabouts, so it won't ever take me that long to find you and deliver the black spot to your hands."

"My pirate days are over, Smiley. I want out, I won't lie to you." He flicked his eyes towards Connie and Smiley chortled.

"Tamed by a woman, my word, that's a poor state you've got yourself into. You were reputedly the best buccaneer of the last of this age of piracy, Edmond Calstock, and that by a long sea-mile. 'Tis a shame. I feel I will not be pitting my wits against you again. End of an era it is, last of our kind and no turning back time. We've all plundered a ship too many, and now they won't rest until we're all swinging. Hawkins brought the end more swiftly with his thirst for blood, may his bones rot! Do you happen to know where he is?"

"If you never found his body, I would say it's decomposing under the waves somewhere."

"So, the last time you saw his face?"

"The day the Rosalie went down."

"Well I respect you, Earnest Eddie that I do. Listen here, go seek your fortune in the New World, but just remember… if I find no treasure then I'm coming for you."

With the uttermost good-timing, Jim came rushing through the tavern door and called, "Mr. Calstock, sir!" Upon casting his eyes in all directions, they finally landed on the group in the corner. He came rushing straight over. "Mr. Calstock, sir, I've come for your sea chest. They're piping the passengers aboard now sir, you don't have long."

The three pirates were already leaving through the side door. Smiley turned back for one last look at Eddie. "Let's hope our paths never cross again, my boy!" And then he was gone, through the door, and to where next Eddie and Connie couldn't care less. They sprang to their feet and rushed with the young man to collect the chest. All of a sudden, Connie was more eager to leave England behind than ever before.

Chapter 23

THEY COULDN'T WAIT TO LEAVE the Minerva Inn and get to the ship. With their bill settled and young Jim bringing their chest on a borrowed cart, they raced towards the dock. When they had climbed the Barbican hill and were descending the other side, the ships in harbor came into full sight and a thrill of excitement washed over Connie. She could feel the same in Eddie, as he hastened their steps and threw constant smiles her way. They were so close to freedom; surely nothing could stop them now.

The road that ran along the seafront overflowed with people. Dotted along the way, many wheelbarrows and carts carried wares for sale from cockles to lace and colorful cloth. Her eyes darted everywhere wanting to soak it all in and miss nothing. On the left of them the sea, to the right a tall grass bank, and everywhere around them people.

The crowd gathered around the *Adventurer's* boarding gangplank was so huge that Connie was overwhelmed. The sky swarmed with screaming gulls, their squawking and crooning fighting for dominance over the noise of the docks. Hawkers cried their wares encouraging custom with their nearly unintelligible words. "Cockles, mussels, all alive this very morning," cried one. "Cream filberts, sorghum candy," cried another. Connie squeezed Eddie's hand tight, fearful he would let her go. He smiled down at her, and then raised her hand to his mouth and kissed it. "No going back now, Connie love."

"It won't sink will it?" she asked, looking at the stunning merchant ship before them.

Eddie laughed, and kissed her hand again. "She's a beauty. Three masted, square rigged, and a whole 280 tons. She's sturdy and I'm told she handles well on the waves. You have nothing to fear; only the worst of storms would cause her any damage, and this is not the season for them."

Connie craned her neck back and looked at the sky as if to make sure. The clear light blue was punctuated by rows of white, fluffy clouds, all racing wherever the wind was taking them. So bright a day was it that a merry spirit and a sprightly step was installed in all.

She took a deep breath, thrilled though she was for the new adventure, negative thoughts still bombarded her relentlessly. Even now, as they inched closer to the gangplank, part of her brain urged her to turn around and run. Run from the unknown, run from Eddie (who she still wholeheartedly believed was a pirate to his core) and run from the woman she had become. If a way to travel to the past existed, she'd embark on it without hesitation. She would return to save Polly, and then she'd ensure she never returned to Burr Island and Bigbury-on-Sea, no matter what Eddie did. If she never returned then she would never have that cliff-top confrontation with Joseph, and he'd still be alive. Ifs, buts and wishes never made a dream come true her mother had told her often, and remember always, she had added, that daydreaming brings nothing but disappointment. An overwhelming yearning to speak with her mother, and share the news of her adventure with her, hit Connie hard. For a moment, she hoped Heaven was a real place and that her parents would be able to share her journey with her by watching from above. They had both been born and bred in Bigbury, and this would appear as exciting to them as it did to her she was sure.

Connie was eventually pulled out of her reverie when she realized she couldn't understand what the people around her were saying. She tugged on Eddie's hand to make him look at her, and once his attention was gained knocked her head to the side, where a group of people were chattering away with great excitement.

Eddie leant towards her ear. "Nearly all the passengers are either Dutch or German," he whispered. Connie's eyes opened wide and she looked about her with more interest.

"Protestants?" she mouthed, and Eddie nodded. She had a new respect for the people who surrounded her. It wasn't the hope of riches that took them on this voyage, it was their faith.

"Where has the sea chest gone?" asked Connie.

"Jim was instructed to pass it to the ship's crew, who will have taken it to the other end of the ship were the goods are loaded, see…" He pointed along the ship. Another gangplank, one (that to her horror) held no rope-rails, was busy with sailors carrying all manner of goods on their shoulders. "Someone will take it to our cabin," Eddie finished.

"With the rest of our things?"

"No, they went into the hold earlier; we won't see them again until we dock in Pennsylvania."

They moved forward again, and now stood feet away from the plank. "Who's that?" asked Connie. On deck, welcoming the passengers aboard stood three men in smart uniforms, but one was particularly distinguished.

"That's Captain John Meirion, the two next to him are the First Mate and the Quartermaster."

In contrast to the other sailors, who wore loose fitting white knee-length breeches and fairly tight-fitting blue and white striped waistcoats, these three men wore clothes that clearly set them apart as gentlemen. John Meirion wore a dark blue coat with rows of brass buttons, which sat snuggly over his tight-fitting white leggings and his blue waistcoat. Even his tri-corn hat was the exact same color as his waistcoat and jacket. And beyond his clothes the man held himself in such a posture as to inspire awe and admiration from Connie, for such a man surely knew exactly who he was and his very presence filled her with a sense of being in very capable hands.

Having been welcomed aboard, Connie and Eddie followed a young lad who led them to their cabin. "Look after us, me laddo," said Eddie, and as the boy turned to leave Eddie pressed a shilling in his hand. "Top of the mornin' to ya, and many thanks. Me names Patty, and I'll be happy to check in on ya every day." He tipped his hand to his blue woolen cap, and then went running off, no doubt to escort another family and gain a few more coins.

"This is a small room, but it is actually larger than I expected. Although to be honest, I wasn't sure what it would be like. But look, besides beds we have a table and chairs and even a place to stow our clothes."

"This *cabin* has two *bunks* and yes it is a good size but then it was meant for a larger family than ours."

"It was?"

"Yes, I'm afraid I had to bribe one of the Dutch families to give it up, the people due to be in 'ere are now spread throughout the other family cabins."

"Oh, Eddie, is everything only bought with money?"

"They gave it up readily, grateful for the money... and no, before you interrupt, not a gold doubloon, but still a good amount that they were most pleased with. It was either offer a family money or Captain Meirion wouldn't take us, no empty bunks he said."

"So you had no choice."

"This was meant to be, can't you feel it?"

She smiled at him. "As a matter of fact I can!"

Eddie swung Connie in his arms, tipped her backwards and gave her a kiss that took her breath away.

At first, she melted at his touch and her stomach jumped and lurched in excitement, but eventually she pulled herself away from her passionate pirate. "Be still, Eddie Calstock, I want to be on deck and watch Plymouth as we sail out of the Sound."

"Umm, let's stay here, for I would rather look at you any day."

"Eddie, come on," she laughed knocking him away. "Sailing might be old hat to you, but it truly is the most wonderful adventure for me!"

"Oh... fair lady... how can I refuse you?"

"Good, then let me take my shawl from the chest for it was breezy up there, and then we shall wave farewell to England forever."

"Connie?"

"Yes?" Connie unlocked the chest and opened it, moving her new purchases aside until she found the gifted tweed shawl. "What is it?" she asked as she stood up with the warm material over her arm.

"Sit on the bunk there a moment, I have something to confess, and I must get it off my chest before another moment passes."

Connie's heart thudded, "What now?" she asked with heavy anticipation and an exaggerated sigh.

He knelt on the floor by her knees. She clasped her hands tightly together.

"First, you know… but I must repeat and be sure you understand that I love you. There I have said it as clear as can be."

Connie sighed and gave a nervous laugh. "Is that all? I thought you were going to tell me something dreadful!"

"Well I must admit that answer is not entirely what I'd have hoped for when I declared myself to a woman."

"I'm sorry, Eddie." For exactly what she was sorry for she didn't elaborate and he took it to mean she was sorry she did not return his sentiments.

"I didn't mention it to put you under any pressure, only to reinforce the fact that my regard for you is sincere and genuine and if I've misled you, 'tis only because I feared to lose you."

"And what, pray tell, have you lied about?"

"I never said I lied, you are (as always) hasty to judge me. Oh I know, I know, I see *that* look, but I have sworn to you of my change and in that I am most determined. No, it isn't that I've lied, just not fully disclosed all the facts. And now that we are safely aboard the *Adventurer* – what an apt name for us! Well then, now we are on board I have something to confess."

"Oh good heavens, Eddie, get on with it! If we set sail and I miss the farewells all because you chose this very precise moment to come clean, well I don't think I'll forgive you in a hurry!"

He burst out laughing, and laughed good and hard. "Oh, Connie," he said swiping at his wet cheeks, "you're the girl for me and that's the truth."

"And…" she said shaking her head, but she was smiling.

"As it happens, the legend of the Delilah Diamond is no myth."

"The diamond is real?" And now Connie sat up straight and leaned forward. "But you said you never touched it!"

"Indeed, I never laid a finger on it. But my eyes caressed it many a time, superstition prevented me from touching it, though I sorely wanted to. It was Hawkins that handled it, under my watchful eye."

"And this diamond is with the treasure? The treasure that you gave Smiley the map to?" her voice rose a pitch with each word.

"Do you know that you sway in your emotions and your decisions more easily than corn in the wind? One moment, you don't want anything to do with pirate booty, the next you're all eager for its knowledge. Sometimes I can barely keep up with your thoughts."

Connie slumped onto the bunk. "Don't think harshly of me, it's only that the diamond carries such mystery about it. I don't wish it for myself. And anyway you have now given the map away, so unless you have memorized the coordinates, can ready a vessel straight away, and gather yourself a crew… why then it is lost to you anyway."

Eddie grinned at her, his eyes sparkled and she could see the glee of his secrets. "Tell me!" she urged.

He opened his new jacket and pointed to the silk lining. "Inside here lies the real map!"

"You had two maps?"

"Yes indeed, so maybe I do have brains after all, eh? And now you know why I kept hold of my old torn coat."

Connie nodded.

"The other map will lead Smiley to a small chest filled only with pieces of eight. The contents will not cover the expense of his voyage," laughed Eddie.

Connie got up and started pacing the minute cabin, he could see the cogs of her brain working, and when she spun to face him, he was ready for the blast.

"He'll come looking for us! You know he will. He'll take the pieces of eight as an insult and he'll set about tracking us down. What have you done, Eddie, but put a death warrant upon both our heads! What about our New World? What about the farm and the apple trees I planned to plant? What about the children we're going to have?"

For a moment he almost fell over. "The children we're going to have?" he asked and his voice was deeply searching.

She pinned him with her stare. "Well, we're adopting aren't we?"

Disappointment flooded his face, and she felt guilty for more reasons than one.

"I don't intend to go for the treasure. I've only told you, so that should something happen to me you know where the map is, and if you're not well taken care of, well then you may become a treasure hunter and live the rest of your days in luxury. I gave you my word that my pirate days are over. When will you ever believe me?"

"It's hard to believe you when you carry a treasure map in your coat lining, and when you rashly deceive a blood-thirsty pirate." Her words were flat, but soft with disappointment. "And what of Hawk-Eye, why didn't he demand you give him the map?"

"That one-eyed pirate has the most astounding memory; he doesn't need a copy of it. I created the map for myself."

"So, he's probably going after the diamond right now?"

"He'll first have to find a new ship and crew, which will take time, as thirty doubloons is only half of what he would need to buy a new ship. But yes, when he's ready he'll go for the treasure without a doubt."

"Why did you bury it anyway? Why not just bring it straight back to England?"

"The diamond is widely searched for at the moment, we couldn't try to sell it without people knowing that we had stolen it. Hawkins came up with the idea of hiding it and going back for it in a few years. Besides that… we…"

"Yes?"

"Well, we never told the rest of the crew about it."

"Who have I married?" Connie put her hand on her knee and began tapping her foot.

Eddie grabbed her hands in his. "I'm a changed man, I promise."

Trust did not come easy to her, but she had to start somewhere. "Can we go upstairs now?" asked Connie standing up.

"We can go up the companionway, and join the others on the main deck."

"Sea terms?"

"Nautical terms."

Connie grinned and took the elbow he offered her.

In the short time they had been below, the cloud cover had increased and turned dark gray. The deck was crowded with passengers all waving goodbye to Plymouth, as the ship gracefully pulled away from the docks. Connie's chest was a-flutter with excitement. "We won't be able to reach the rails," she moaned.

"Come on," Eddie took her hand and started pulling her forward. "It's far better to look forward than to look behind. From now on, you and I, Mrs. Calstock, are only ever going to look forward. Agreed?"

He glanced down at her as he pulled her on. "Agreed!" she answered with a laugh. They made it to bow of the ship, and here the crowd thinned out.

"What's that?" she asked.

"The island you mean?"

"Yes."

"It's called Drake's Island, after the privateer Sir Francis Drake."

"Who was he?"

"You don't know?"

She shook her head.

"Well, one hundred and fifty years ago he set sail from Plymouth – just like us, in a grand galleon named the *Golden Hind*. It is believed he was the first man to sail right around the world."

"And they named the island after him, did he live there then?"

"No, it has been a prison for many a long year."

Connie shivered, and Eddie tightened his grip. Needless to say the pair of them would rather not go there.

Chapter 24

MOST OF THE MEN were already on board, only a few had remained to the last, including Snake-Eye, Spike and Vera Brave. Smiley appeared in the doorway, Queenie curled in his arms and purred as he stroked her.

"Jump to it, you old sea-dogs, it's time to leave this god-forsaken piece of rock and get back to what we do best."

"Aye-aye, Cap'n," echoed from all around.

"You should leave 'er behind," snarled Snake-Eye as he and Spike passed Smiley, thumbing over his shoulder. When Snake-Eye had passed through the door, Brave approached Smiley with heavy steps. She squared her chin at him and thrust her hands on her hips with elbows wide, her fingers deliberately lingering on her cutlass hilt.

"I fight as well as any man," she spat, "and well you it know, Cap'n."

"'Tis true and the only reason I let you sail with us, even though women are the cause of all bad luck! Get you gone now before I change my mind."

Brave tapped her tri-corn hat and nearly sent it flying off her head. She grinned, displaying her blackened teeth, before leaving the small inn for the adventure of the seas once more.

The twitch in Old Jimmy Peg-Leg's left eye fluttered with speed, as it was prone to do when he was stressed. Smiley had already told him he would be left behind to keep the inn in order until he returned.

"Peg!" barked Smiley.

"Yes, Cap'n Smiley, sir?" replied Peg, shuffling across the room, his wooden stump sounding mighty hollow against the cold stone flags of the floor in the empty room.

"Your share of the plunder keep you going?"

"Yes, Cap'n, it will indeed."

Smiley regarded his old sailor mate with a furrowed brow. Many a man would take this opportunity to line his own pockets and leave Smiley to return to empty coffers. Peg looked back up at him, as honest as any pirate could be. He lived by the Code, and would not break it, of this Smiley was sure. He breathed easy.

"Look after Queenie for me, if anything happens to her I'll have your head!"

"You're not taking her with you this time, Cap'n?"

Smiley stroked the black cat for a moment and then handed her into Peg's arms. "She's gotten old, Peg, she won't have any sea-legs about her any more, and if she can't catch rats what's her worth?" He didn't mention that Polly had loved Queenie like a child, and that he could no more look at the cat because of the memories she stirred.

Peg, wise old man, didn't answer, he knew the Cap'n loved this black ball of fluff and he shouldn't say anything against her.

"Do you think the treasures' there, Cap'n?"

"I won't know until we find it. It seemed to me that Earnest Eddie loved that fisherman's wife through and through and would want her safety. With that in mind I don't think he fooled us."

"When might you return, Cap'n?"

"The winds of fortune will be the deciders of that."

"Aye-aye Cap'n, may your sails be ever full."

Smiley nodded at his oldest serving crew member, "Aye, and may the treasures be bountiful!"

Peg watched Smiley stomp away towards the secret passageway between the inn and the caves. Behind Peg the ghosts of Tom Crocker and Polly Fists stood, two broken people who had both had their lives snatched away too early on this piece of rock called Burr Island. Tom's apparition slipped into the fireplace, but Polly's rose and floated down the passage after her one true love.

Time would delay and be slow to pass, for Smiley would never be able to bring himself to return to Bigbury-on-Sea to the memory of his one and only Polly. Only on his death, and commanded by a new captain, would the Flying Angel sail into the English Channel again and return to the Pilchard Inn, to find old Peg long gone from pleurisy.

Chapter 25

June 17th, 1727

On the ship Adventurer, sailing for Pennsylvania

CONSCIENCE ACCUSES ITS CARRIER and becomes a dreadful thing – if its extent is high and the deed of regret is low. Conscience urges a person to do no wrong and if that urge is ignored it declares war upon that person's soul and causes all manner of uncomfortable thoughts to lower and humble them. Connie's conscience had given her little peace since the storm had shipwrecked the Rosalie on Burr Island beach. She wondered how she would bear the weight of it. For herself she might have succumbed to regretful melancholy and wasted her life. Her hands fleetingly rested upon the skirts over her middle as she thought about how tender her breasts had become. Sometimes in life, the most unexpected things occur, and they demand to take precedence over conscience. Care and nurture must come to center place and take their places there in a most zealously determined way. Years of feeling worthless must fade away.

All around them she heard the exuberant chatter and laughter of the passengers. Beyond the foreign babble drifted a song of sailors as they hoisted the sails and tied their ropes.

There was a distant land, upon a foreign strand
In a rough old cabin in the shade
Sat a toiler who, tho' he'd roughed it through
Quite a hard-earned for–tune there had made
Seated around were his com–rades
Till our heave–ho broke the spell
Now boys, one more 'ere I leave you he cried
For you know quite well
There's a big ship sailin' in the mornin'

The song made her smile and she snuggled in closer to Eddie. He in turn tightened his hold on his new wife.

The gathering wind picked up speed, and with it carried large dark gray clouds over them. The sudden gale caused the sails to billow and flutter, the sound so loud to be as a thousand-fold the crackle and snap of the laundered sheets behind the house on washday. Blasts of wind rocked the ship, as the clouds opened up and began to empty their heavy load over the Devonshire coast. Rain splashed their faces and drenched the deck in moments. Passengers ran hither and thither, laughing and calling to one another as they scurried inside. The crew, already busy, leapt into action. Blasts of a whistle called them this way and that as they tugged on ropes and directed the sails.

Connie made to move to shelter, but Eddie grabbed her hand. "Stay," he urged, his smile wide and eyes all a sparkle. She relented to his merry spirit and stayed within his arms. He turned her around so they were both facing forward, his body her shield against the storm that was brewing. She leaned back against him and took comfort from his warmth. His arms tightened around her waist. A sense of wellbeing washed over her and she sank into the giddy feeling of being treasured and cared for. Out of the blue, the comprehension that she was finally 'home' and in the place where she belonged engulfed her. Tears ran unchecked down her cheeks and mingled with raindrops, as she realized that dreams do (sometimes) come true.

She turned her head slightly to speak towards his ear so that he might hear her against the din of the waves and scurrying sailors. "They won't turn us back for shore will they?"

He leaned down and nuzzled into her neck. "No my love, they won't. This is but a mild summer storm and will soon pass." She sighed in relief. She didn't want to go back, not even one step. A New World was before them and she knew she would fight for it with every breath in her body.

The *Adventurer* forged ahead through the rolling waves, rising and falling as gracefully as a bird in flight. Other passengers were feeling seasick already, but Connie kept her eyes on the horizon and felt nothing but the thrill of the unknown. She loved this ship that carried them forward into a new life.

As if he'd heard her thoughts Eddie announced, "Our future lies out there."

"Will it bring us happiness, do you think?"

His hands moved to her shoulders and he turned her around. "The world is whatever we make of it, my girl. We'll endeavor to be content wherever destiny takes us. I promise you, I'll do everything I can to ensure you receive the happiness you deserve."

His words brought great clarity for Connie, it was as if the closeness to death had refreshed the world and everything was crystal clear and stark, vibrant and pulsing with life. She was at a crossroads and she had a decision to make. This choice wavered on the pinnacle of her life. She needed to determine who she was. Polly's voice came to her ears… those who hesitate are already lost. She was brave, she was adventurous but more importantly she realized she was a woman in love.

Connie knew in that moment she had to make a life-altering decision. Should she remain encased in cruel memories that shrouded her heart in misery in order to protect it? Or could she let go of the past? And if she took a chance and he turned out to be like the other men she'd met in her life… well then, she would have to deal with disappointment and hurt again.

Her gaze drank in the sparkle of hope within his eyes as he willed her to respond.

And just like that – she knew. No doubts, just sudden unbelievable clarity. She would take that risk. If life turned out to be a disappointment, well she would face it and forge a new path forward. But for now she wanted love, honest, unfiltered affection that brought with it a promise of happiness.

She wrapped her cold fingers around his wet face that seemed to have aged ten years in a matter of weeks. "We'll be the happiest people on Earth, for I love you Edmond Calstock, and I will do until the day I die."

The warmth and truth of her statement set both their hearts on fire.

"Oh, my sweetheart!" He pulled her into his arms and squeezed her tightly against him as his lips reached for hers. That kiss seared a connection between them. Completely oblivious to the rain they molded into one spirit. Never again would they face their fears and struggles alone. From this day forth they would be united in everything – whatever that might be. For *love* is the triumphant seal between two people who promise to give of themselves for the rest of their lives.

Thank you for reading.

If you enjoyed Connie's story could I please encourage you to leave me a review? Without reviews a book never succeeds, and I would really appreciate your endorsement and support. Many thanks.

If you would like to receive updates by receiving my email newsletter, please sign up at [SendFox](https://sendfox.com)

In my newsletter will be updates about my books, book competitions, a book review from me and eBooks that are on offer or free by other authors. The newsletter is only quarterly, so only 4 a year ☺ no spam or sharing of details.

If you have been affected by issues in this fictional account, help is available.

UK https://www.victimsupport.org.uk/crime-info/types-crime/domestic-abuse

US https://ncadv.org/get-help

Appendix

I would like to give thanks and acknowledgments to the following, these websites and books were a vital part of my research.

Burgh Island Hotel
Having already picked Bigbury-on-Sea as the setting for my book, I was over the moon when I first discovered Burgh Island has a history of pirates and smuggling. This was the first I had heard of it, on the Burgh Island Hotel website.

https://www.burghisland.com

Book Resource
A General History of the Pyrates: From their firstd of Providence to the Present time, by Daniel Defoe. Picked up an eBook from Amazon for the amazing price of £0.49! The most unbelievably informative chronicles of pirates for a giveaway price! An author's dream resource!

https://www.amazon.co.uk/dp/B01IVR855K

Pilchards
'The Cornish Good Seafood Guide' offered a great look at the historical fishing of pilchards along the Cornwall and Devon coastline.

https://www.cornwallgoodseafoodguide.org.uk/cornish-fishing/history-of-the-cornish-fishing-industry.php

Census

I spent a great deal of time trying to find out whether Bigbury had a lord or gentleman from the manor, in 1727. About to give up after finding nothing, I finally (by accident while looking for something else) stumbled across GENUKI and a tiny article within mentioning past keepers of the hamlets manor, delighted!

https://www.genuki.org.uk/big/eng/DEV/Bigbury

Ghost Story of pirate Tom Crocker

I first found mention of Burgh Island's ghost from Weird Tales Radio Show, and was instantly intent on slipping the story of the ghost into my novel.

https://www.urbanfantasist.com/weird-tales-radio-show/friday-13th-ghost-story

More valuable details about Tom Crocker were then found on Smuggling – South Hams, Devon blog.

https://smugglingsouthhams.wordpress.com/tom-crocker

Pirate Clothing - & other things

The Elizabethan-era website was like finding a diamond in an internet full of semi-precious stones. The details are great, but so are the reasons behind them. Great research resource.

https://www.elizabethan-era.org.uk/pirate-clothing.htm

Smugglers

There is so much great information on this site alone, that I feel I should almost write another story just about smugglers!

http://www.smuggling.co.uk/history_crossing.html

Immigration to America

I would like to thank the Historical Society of Pennsylvania for their great website with its wonderful historical content. From there I was able to see the name of the ship leaving Plymouth in 1727, the captain and how many souls were on board.

http://digitalhistory.hsp.org/pafrm/doc/memorial-against-non-english-immigration-december-1727

There is such an amazing wealth of knowledge to be gained for free nowadays if the researcher endeavors to look. Here's to the modern age of technology that means I don't have to spend my life traveling from library to library and taking years to write a book instead of months. My sincere thanks to all 'posters' of information.

Author Information

If you'd like to know more about my books, please check out my web.

http://www.tntraynor.uk

You can also find me on Facebook.

https://www.facebook.com/groups/292316321513651

Or Twitter: @tracy_traynor

If you enjoyed this book you might also enjoy one of my other books:

Women of Courage Series

https://www.amazon.com/Women-Courage-4-Book/dp/B091TTXQ6V

MULTI AWARD WINNING SERIES

Standalone Stories with a theme of courage and love

WOMEN OF COURAGE

1912 - 1985	1904 - 1905	2020	1958	1666
Inspired by the life of Moira Smith	Inspired by the Welsh Revival	A Love Story	A story of hope	A story of faith

Young Adult Fantasy, Born to Be, series

https://www.amazon.com/dp/B01C1UDQKC

Printed in Great Britain
by Amazon